# *The Illustrated History of* BRADFORD'S SUBURBS

# *The Illustrated History of*
# BRADFORD'S SUBURBS

Michael Birdsall, Gina Szekely, Peter Walker

First published in Great Britain in 2002 by
The Breedon Books Publishing Company Limited
Breedon House, 3 The Parker Centre,
Derby, DE21 4SZ.



**Acknowledgements**

This book has only been made possible by the kind help of many different people and organisations. Special thanks must go to all the staff in the Reference and Local Studies Department of Bradford Central Library for their usual help and assistance; Mr and Mrs Booth for their permission to use the photographs of the late Jack Booth; the late Mabel Bruce; Anne and David Birdsall for the photographs and transport around the district, and the inspiring works of local historians and history societies within Bradford. Thanks also to all our families for their help and support.

ISBN 1 85983 309 8

Printed and bound by Butler & Tanner, Frome, Somerset, England.

Cover printing by Lawrence-Allen Colour Printers, Weston-super-Mare, Somerset, England.

# CONTENTS

# Introduction

THE Bradford district, with its many, often disparate, suburbs can be considered to be almost unique in its geographical make up. The relatively compact city centre lies in what can best be described as a bowl, fanned out around the impressive Gothic City Hall at its heart. The outlying townships, villages and hamlets, which have gradually become immersed into the suburbs of Bradford, are spread across the hills, which rise, often steeply, on three sides of this bowl, and along the valley which leads to Shipley and beyond.

This geography, the steep inclines and the valleys between, led to settlements forming very differently across the district, often in a state of seeming isolation. The 'village ethos' which pervaded self-sufficient communities, settled in remote hamlets, survived for centuries almost untouched by the events and progress being made in the larger townships of Bradford, Bowling, Horton and others. What sense of allegiance to Bradford did the people of Wrose or Thornton hold in days gone by? Both occupy high ground several miles from the centre of town, and could be considered almost cut off from events there. Indeed, it has been noted that in Thornton's case, even a period in England's history as turbulent as the Civil War had virtually no impact on the lives of the people who lived there, despite the almost dire consequences it had for nearby Bradford.

So what were the connections with Bradford for people outside the centre? In 1251 Edmund de Lacy had been granted a charter by Henry III giving the right to hold a market in Bradford every Thursday. So from an early period in history, the inhabitants of many of the outlying regions had at least one reason to come down into the centre. Livestock and produce would have been sold or traded for wares not readily available 'up in the hills'.

The other main reason for members of the more 'noted' families to travel into Bradford in the Middle Ages was to attend mass on Sunday at Bradford parish church (now the Cathedral). Bradford parish extended 14 miles around the church, the only other church standing at Haworth, and as the journey into Bradford would inevitably have been long and even hazardous, the market also came to be held on Sunday, in the churchyard, so as to halve the number of treks into the town. Did this coming together for business and religious purposes give the people of, say, Allerton and Eccleshill, a larger sense of 'community', of being Bradfordians? Probably not, as many areas retained a fierce independence right up to their eventual incorporation with Bradford in the 19th century.

The Domesday Book tells us that before the Norman Conquest, a man by the name of Gamel owned Bradford and six dependent outlying 'berewicks' or farmsteads. The Manor of Bradford was granted to Ilbert de Lacy following the conquest and was subsequently long held by the de Lacy family, but the many districts covered in this book fell under different manors, with different ruling families. The Bolling family had Bowling; the Plumptons are associated with Idle, while Eccleshill was for many years part of the Manor of Wakefield.

Daniel Defoe toured the north of England in 1720, and was impressed by Leeds and the industry of the people of Halifax, but gave barely a mention to Bradford. The town was not prospering at the time, and the first workhouse for the poor of Bradford was opened at Barker End. The manufacture of worsted was on the rise yet it was still very much a cottage industry. The late 1700s saw a huge boost to trade in Bradford with the opening of the Bradford Canal, which linked the town centre with the Leeds-Liverpool Canal. Transport was all-important for the movement of wool and worsted products, and the canal added to the turnpike roads which had been opened earlier in the century and which cut across such districts as Dudley Hill and Bradford Moor. Such improvements to transport could only help trade in Bradford, and by the middle of the 19th century the town was booming. The Low Moor Company and the Bowling Iron Works were already well established by then, as were several collieries, including Bunkers Hill at Bradford Moor.

Factories and mills were being constructed in Bradford at a furious pace – not just in the centre of town but all across the district. Areas such as Idle, Eccleshill, Thornton and Laisterdyke quickly gained their own mills, providing work for both locals and jobseekers from further afield. The rise of the factory system was not welcomed with open arms by all of Bradford's workers, however, as some saw it as the end of their traditional ways of making a living. For generations, people across the district had worked at home. Traditional weavers' cottages still survive in many outlying villages. In 1826 a mob from Bradford Moor joined in an attack on a mill in North Wing, which left two protesters dead. However, nothing could stop the tide of industrialisation that was sweeping across the West Riding, and Bradford was inundated with people arriving in the town seeking employment in the numerous mills. The population rocketed during the 19th century. In 1801 it stood at just over 6,000. By the mid-point of the century it had reached over 103,000 and at the census of 1891 it was recorded as 216,361.

Such a huge increase in population inevitably led to a massive build up in housing developments across the district. Open spaces were quickly eaten up as rows of terrace houses, shops, public buildings and even more works premises were erected. Girlington, for example, was almost entirely the product of this process of development, for prior to the 19th century it was little more than an area of wasteland with the odd farmstead dotted about. Developments gradually spread along all the main routes out of the city centre. Up Thornton, Manchester, Leeds and Great Horton Roads communities merged, boundaries blurred and Bradford expanded. The administrative boundaries of Bradford had already been altered when the town was granted a Charter of Incorporation in 1847, bringing together the ancient townships of Bowling, Horton, Manningham and, of course, Bradford itself.

Outlying communities such as Eccleshill and Idle continued to be self-governed via local boards, which oversaw the provision of schools, the collection of rates and so on. Such independence of local government was not long lived, however, as Bradford gradually consumed its outlying districts. Allerton, Heaton, Frizinghall and Thornbury were added to Bradford's control in 1882; Eccleshill, Idle, North Bierley, Thornton and Tong in 1899.

Further improvements to the district's transport system began in 1882 with the opening of a half-hourly horse-drawn tram service between the town centre and Manningham Park. By 1884, steam trams were operating up Manchester Road and by 1897 electricity was powering trams up Bolton Road towards Eccleshill and up Great Horton Road. By the early 1900s, many of Bradford's outlying districts were connected to the tram system, meaning that people living in almost any area within the district could now easily reach the town centre. Railways were also quite accessible to many people. From the 1860s onwards railway lines had been constructed across much of Bradford, and stations had been opened in many places. It may seem strange to youngsters today that places such as Thackley, Great Horton, Idle and Windhill once boasted their own stations.

Like the district's many small railway stations, Bradford's local churches and chapels have been subject to demolition, dereliction and modern conversion. William Cudworth's works and the 19th-century trade directories define a district by its religious character and fervour. This is not of paramount importance today. There has been a shift in religion's cultural emphasis, but not an absolute decline within the local communities of Bradford. Indeed, as Tony Jowitt points out in 'The Pattern of Religion in Victorian Bradford' in *Victorian Bradford* (1982), many churches and chapels were built in the late 1800s as a response to church-chapel rivalries and prestige building, rather than actual congregational needs. This left problems of maintenance poverty for some, rather than actual congregational decline. Studies also show a process of religious fragmentation, a growth in the number of denominations, which reflects the cosmopolitanism of Bradford and its central suburbs, and the continual growth of sects such as the spiritualists. The population of Bradford has also acquired religious freedoms, political and social rights and opportunities for secular leisure activities, which have shifted emphasis away from this central Victorian value. Today there are still buildings for religious worship within most suburbs, with active congregations of all ages, but their diversity defies the concise definition commonly used in 19th-century township accounts, hence the lack of emphasis in this brief introductory study.

People from overseas have long made Bradford their home. In the mid-19th century many Irish settled in the city, soon followed by

Bradford historian William Cudworth. His book *Round About Bradford* inspired this work. *(Bradford Libraries)*

German wool merchants, who built large, impressive warehouses close to the town centre in an area that quickly became known as Little Germany. Many of these Germans made their homes in the smart villas off Manningham Lane, starting a tradition of multi-culturalism in the Manningham area. After World War Two Bradford welcomed many families from eastern Europe. Little Horton, in particular, was home to a well-established Polish Club, which helped keep alive the language and culture of the homeland for future generations. The 1950s and 1960s saw many south Asians moving into the district, lured by the promise of work in the city's mills. Once again Manningham became host to a large and thriving community of people from differing backgrounds and cultures. Today, many other areas within Bradford have large Asian communities. All these citizens have contributed to the rich diversity that characterises Bradford's many districts today, the beginnings of which were acknowledged by local historians such as

William Cudworth at the very inception of the 19th century industrial city of Bradford.

Writing a book that looks at Bradford's suburbs is not a particularly easy exercise. The selection process alone was a difficult one. The question that will always be levelled at the authors is 'Why isn't my area in the book?' Shipley, Keighley and Ilkley, with their satellite communities, for example, are excluded because all three are large enough to warrant similar publications of their own. We couldn't possibly hope to do justice to any of them in the few pages that are available. Once we had eliminated these from our reckoning, we pored over maps of the district and from the resulting list we selected as many villages and townships as we felt able to cover. If your particular area is not included all we can do is apologise.

The aims of this book are not to produce the definitive history and description of a given area. The chapters are intended to be an introduction to the local histories of these places with a brief description of what is happening there now. We have endeavoured to include further reading lists for those wishing to take a more in-depth interest in a particular area, and many of the books cited are published by local history groups following in the footsteps of local historians such as William Cudworth, who inspired this study. Their works have proved an invaluable source of reference and interest and it is through their diligence, care and enthusiasm that so much information is now available, especially regarding the more recent past.

Local history is a burgeoning subject and interest in it has increased with the development of new technology, which has given worldwide virtual access to local communities, their news and history. It has also provided new ways of preserving and promoting local history and quite a few groups now have their own internet web sites.

We hope that you enjoy reading this book and that it encourages you to further explore 'round about' this fascinating city of Bradford.

# Allerton

ALLERTON lies three miles west of Bradford. It was incorporated with Bradford borough in April 1882. The Domesday Book calls it Alretune or Alretone, which originates from the Saxon *aller*, based on a profusion of alder trees once growing in the area, and *ton* meaning enclosure or homestead, which also refers to the Saxon *tun* or *tunes*, which were hedges made to protect dwellings. At the time of the Norman Conquest, Allerton was part of the Manor of Bolton, having been given to Ilbert de Lacy by William the Conqueror for his assistance in subduing the area. Subsequently, the manor was at various times in the hands of the following families: the Thorntons until 1327; the Bollings (of Bolling Hall); the Tempests; and, until 1794, the Marsdens of Gisburn. It was then conveyed by deed to Benjamin Ferrand of St Ives, near Bingley, for £2,400. The Thorntons and Bollings held manor courts at Allerton. In that time the rents were composed of small sums, with 'the addition of roses'. Cudworth notes that at a court held in 1504, 22 Allerton freeholders appeared and 17-year-old John Aldersley, a ward, was presented holding his land '...by Knight's service and by a yearly rent of 22d and a rose, price one penny.'

Michael McDermott identifies three divisions of the village in the past. The 'top' of the village was formed first, and this is now the Prune Park area. The bottom of the hill came next, and finally the middle of the village, known as the 'copy' area, which it is thought gets its name from the term copyhold tenure, by which an early tenant of the manor could be freed from service on payment of a fee. This area became the site of Well Row Mill in 1862 (later Allerton or Smiths Mill complex) and became the most populated section of the village with the building of back-to-back terrace houses for the workers. It is now what could be described as the centre of Allerton village.

The two main industries of the past were the worsted trade and stone quarrying. Cudworth traces the worsted trade in Allerton back to a Mr Pearson who lived at Street Gap and employed four combers and gave out weaving in the area around. Other well-known weavers and spinners included Joshua Illingworth, Jeremiah Robertshaw, Joseph Wood and James, John and Jonas White. It was after 1750 that Allerton's commercial interests grew, but the most intensive period was 1830–50. By 1845 there were about 240 hand-loom weavers and wool combers. Cudworth reports that twice a week, two large loads of moreen (fabric) were despatched to Bradford, but many weavers were employed by other district manufacturers. Now the old pack horse tracks once used for such journeys are mostly covered with houses. The first mill was erected in Allerton in 1836. It was occupied by Uriah Ackroyd and Jeremiah Robertshaw. At the time of Cudworth's writing there were five working mills in the village, employing over 1,500 hands and turning out products which he claims were the best of any being manufactured in the villages around Bradford.

Allerton's other successful industry was stone quarrying. In 1868, there were 36 quarries. In Cudworth's time most of these had been worked out to leave only 15 in operation. Allerton stone was sent all over England. It was used in the building of the London Law Courts, but by 1922 the stone industry had almost disappeared. Today Allerton's largest employer is the famous Seabrook Potato Crisps Ltd, which had its beginnings after World War Two

Dean House, built in 1605, was the local workhouse at the end of the 1700s and was known locally as the 'Bastille'. It still enjoys some of the original countryside today. *(Gina Szekely)*

as a sideline to a fish and chip shop belonging to Charles Brook and his son Colin, in Great Horton Road. The crisps were delivered to pubs in paper bags with the tops twisted and landlords would try and bribe the young Colin with a beer to leave extra bags, because they were in short supply due to rationing. In 1949, the Brooks founded a new factory in Allerton, converted from the building formerly owned by the old Allerton Liberal Club, and the firm took up its present title. It is now the largest family-run crisp manufacturer in Britain. Apparently, its rather unusual name originates from the misspelling of the late Mr Charles Brook's name (C. Brook) on a packet of holiday photographs which he had just had developed. In the late 1990s, it was feared that the firm might shift all its production to its Girlington plant, reducing the Allerton works to a warehouse, but instead it spent £1 million upgrading its Allerton factory to secure the jobs of around 100 workers.

Allerton Hall once stood in Allerton Lane. It was built by the Firth family in 1777. Joshua Firth was a man of some renown, had a bank and issued what were called 'Firth notes', which he used as payment for the hand-loom weavers of the locality. They could redeem them at the hall. Benjamin Kaye, another occupant, was a master clothier in the cotton trade. He distributed pieces to weave in the surrounding district, and had his market in Manchester. The hall was also host to Charlotte Brontë on one occasion. Unfortunately, it fell into disrepair and was eventually purchased by Bradford Council. It was demolished in 1968. A photograph of it can be seen in *Lost Houses of the West Riding* (see Further Reading). Allerton Lane, once the location of Allerton Hall, has its own ghost called Rebecca. Her beauty was locally renowned and she was betrothed to a man from the Hollingwood Lane area, who is said to have murdered her nearby. She supposedly cried out 'Pity poor Becca!', hence the name of the local bridge, Pitty Beck Bridge. Her ghost is said to have walked Allerton Lane ever since.

Today Allerton can still boast Dean House, built in 1605, probably one of the oldest inhabited houses in Bradford. Named after the builder, Robert Deane, this was the local workhouse at around the end of the 1700s and the local name for the building used to be the 'Bastille', according to Michael McDermott. The date stone also contains a double cross, which denotes land once belonging to the order of St John of Jerusalem. Cudworth notes that, according to a charter roll dated 1617, the Knights of St John had a manor in Allerton called Crosley, which consisted of scattered detached allotments around Crosley Hall, granted to them by 'pious admirers' in the 13th century. Bailey Fold, a small well-built farmhouse of 1612, is famous as the home of Joseph Lister, the local historian of the Civil Wars. A full account of his first-hand experience of the Siege of Bradford can be read in Abraham Holroyd's *Collectanea Bradfordiana*, published in 1873.

In Cudworth's time, Allerton is described as having 'exceptionally pure and bracing air', which is one of the reasons he gives for the longevity of some of the villagers relative to other districts. It also had less crime and drunkenness than other areas and was well known for its musicians and choral singers. When they were not supporting Allerton's very own Glee and Madrigal Society, they went to Bradford to practice with the Old Choral Society. In 1916 the Allerton Free Library was opened on the Annual Walk Day of the village with a procession, band, buns and coffee. It was the gift of Councillor Angus H. Rhodes, Lord Mayor in 1929, who was also a local resident. The first religious building in Allerton to be built was the independent chapel (Little Bethel), built by the local residents in 1814. The first church at Allerton came in 1870 with the

The famous Seabrook Potato Crisps Ltd, founded in Allerton in 1949. *(Gina Szekely)*

Bailey Fold, dating from 1612, was built by Joseph Bailey, builder. It was once the home of Joseph Lister, the historian. *(Gina Szekely)*

Prospect Mill, Allerton, (date unknown). *(Bradford Libraries)*

erection of the mission church, which was used as a Sunday School for St Peter's Church when it opened in 1879.

The tradition of improved air and energetic society must have continued to have some effect on some of the inhabitants and indeed the animals of Allerton, because in 1904 Allerton cricket team (which had begun playing in the 1850s) became the first winners of the prestigious Priestley Cup of the Bradford Cricket League. Between 1977 and 1981, Terry Kimber-Smith became repeatedly world and national title winner for three-wheel motor-cycling and Bess, a racing whippet, competed undefeated in more than 240 races in 1988–90 and, under the name of 'No Comment', won every major competition in the UK.

In 2002, Allerton has similar social problems to other areas and is now quite built up with surrounding housing estates. Nevertheless, it still has its own park, Ladyhill Park, a gift from Sir James and Lady Hill, with panoramic views down to Bradford. Sir James Hill, owner of the local 'Top Mill', was Lord Mayor in 1908–9, chairman of the Tramways Committee and became a baronet in 1916. Allerton has also retained most of the old village green, given to the village in the 1840 Allerton Enclosure Act, which is still used as a recreation ground off Allerton Road. However, it is the countryside around Chellow Dene which continues to give the most pleasure to Allerton inhabitants. It is one of their oldest beauty spots. The two reservoirs here were built between 1842 and 1852, and a £1.3 million scheme begun in the 1990s has restored and enhanced the attractions of the site. Gone are the risks of flooding, the guns and live munitions exposed when the reservoirs were drained. Today, this is once again one of Bradford's scenic leisure attractions and a major wildlife haven. The lower reservoir provides the only home in Yorkshire for the rare rusty back fern, and

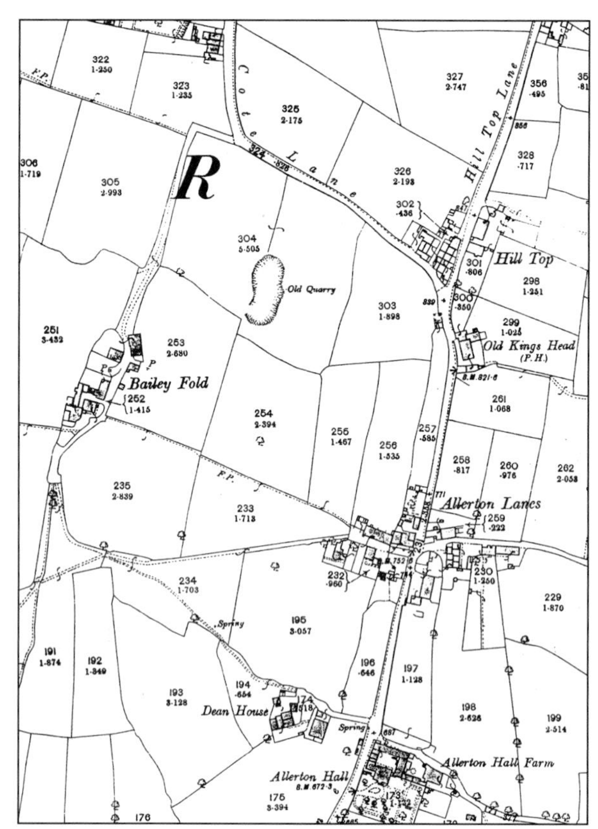


Bailey Fold and Allerton Lanes, shown on a map of the 1890s.

environmental improvements include tree planting, disabled access, picnic tables and a wildfowl island.

**Further Reading**

**Cudworth, William** *Histories of Manningham, Heaton, and Allerton* W. Cudworth, Bradford, 1896.

**Fawcett, Revd Joshua** 'Bradford in The Olden Time' in Abraham Holroyd, *Collectanea Bradfordiana*, 1873.

**McDermott, Michael** *Allerton in Byegone Days* M. McDermott, Bradford, 1989.

**McDermott, Michael** *Allerton Village Past and Present* M. McDermott, Bradford, 1987.

**McDermott, Michael** *West of Bradford* M. McDermott, Bradford, 1991.

**Waterson, Edward and Peter Meadows** *Lost Houses of the West Riding* Jill Raines, York, 1998.

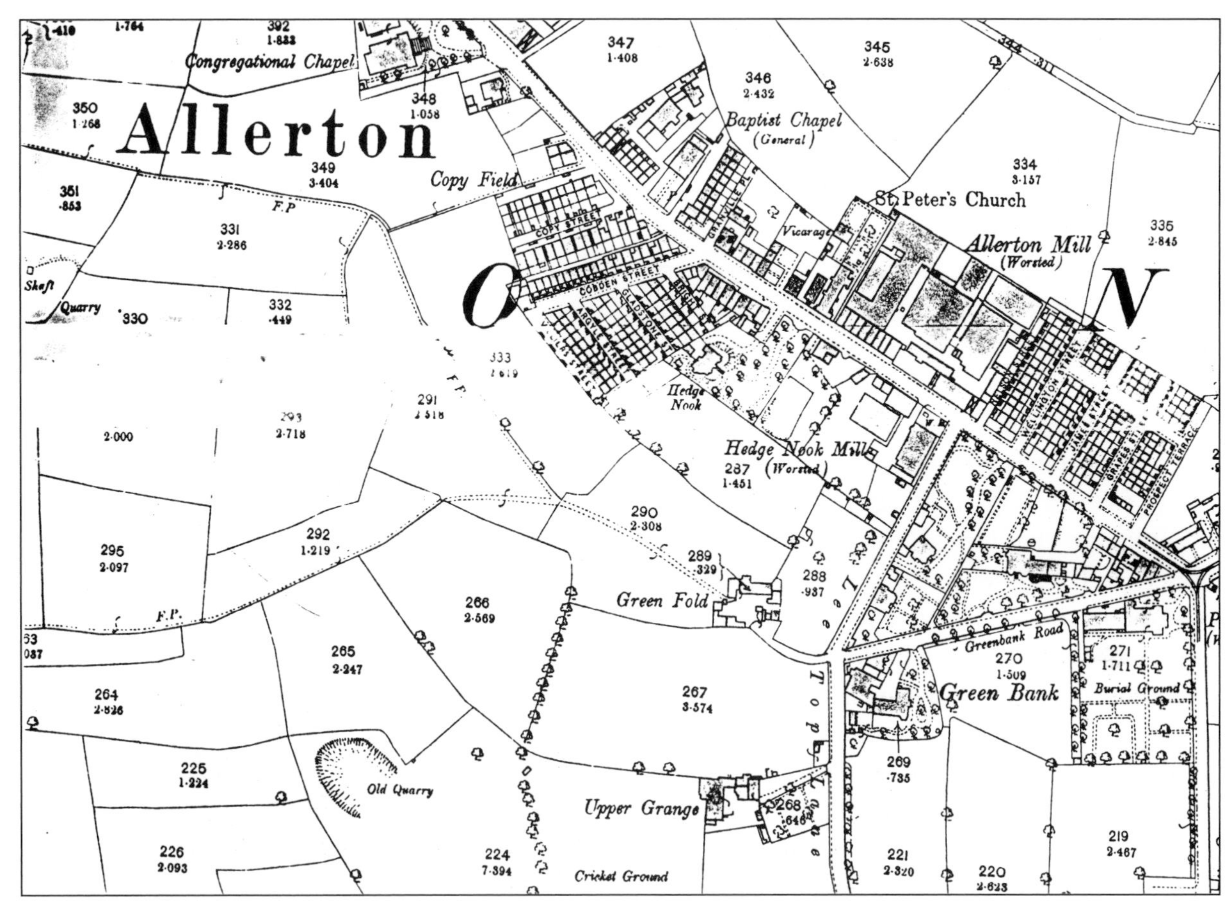

Map of Allerton, *c.*1893.

Bonfire to celebrate the Coronation of 1902. *(Bradford Libraries)*

# Bolton

WILLIAM Cudworth traces the name of Bolton back to two words: *bolle* from early Chaucerian ballads meaning bull, and *ton* the Anglo-Saxon word for town, which reflects the original agricultural character of Bolton. In 1891, Cudworth describes Bolton as still largely rural in character, though with changes in land usage. In the Domesday Book cultivation of land was set at 400 acres, and in 1846 only 226 acres were arable and 450 were kept for meadow and pasture as Bolton helped supply Bradford's growing population with milk and beef.

Bolton is not described as a village but as a township, consisting of scattered clusters of houses in the ancient settlements of Old Bolton, Delph Hill, Hodgson Fold, Low Fold and Bolton Outlanes. The township boundary then followed the line of Bradford Beck, taking in the canal, Frizinghall Mill, the Isle of Man, Idle in the west, Eccleshill in the east and Bradford in the south. It also included a section of Peel Park and New Queen's Road.

In 1800 there were only about 470 people in the township. It had neither a squire, doctor, parson, policeman nor publican, and the people Cudworth describes as sturdy, industrious and independent, with few poor. Among the local landowners, Cudworth mentions the Listers, the Stanhopes, on whose land Bolton Old Hall (1626) was situated, the Rawson family, and the Hodgsons. The Hodgson family's land later passed by marriage to J.A. Jowett and his son John Hodgson Atkinson-Jowett who, in 1891, was the largest landowner in Bolton. He lived at Grove House, built by his father in the Italian style in 1860. Sadly this no longer remains, and the land is now occupied by Hanson and Grove House First Schools. Other yeoman families of early importance include the Walkers, Midgleys, Hemingways and Hollings families and some detail is given by Cudworth about these, including the pedigree of the Atkinson-Jowetts.

Cudworth gets much of his information from the contents of the 'old town's box at Pendragon Castle', known by some locally then as Bolton's town hall and originally a hut constructed on the Saxon 'pen', an enclosure for cattle or sheep. From this information, he tells us of the general opposition to the incorporation of Bolton into Bradford in 1873, as 'the farmers and quarrymen were well

Walnut Tree Farm, Bolton Lane, also known as Bartlett House, Bolton Banks Farm and Walnut House, due to the existence of an ancient walnut tree planted against the house. Built in 1736 by Benjamin and Elizabeth Bartlett. *(Ann Birdsall)*

Cottages in Hodgson Fold, Bolton, now a conservation area. *(Gina Szekely)*

satisfied with things as they were', and resented being taxed for services they did not want or already had. Nevertheless, Bolton did gain some material benefits upon its incorporation in 1873, not the least of these coming from the general improvements in local communications. Bolton roads were improved, especially Bolton Lane, which led from Manningham to Bolton and Peel Park and was once quite a burden to local ratepayers. The construction of Valley Road and Queen's Road also helped the local economy, which also included coal mining and stone quarrying.

Bolton Old Hall is said to have been at the site of the former 'town' of Bolton and Cudworth notes the names of two adjoining meadows in his time which testify to this tradition and which were named Town Fields. The date of the hall, Cudworth assumes, is from a stone inscribed T.W. 1627, the initials being for Thomas Walker, from whom the Stanhopes allegedly purchased the estate. The hall was said to have been haunted by a ghost and safeguards against evil such as horseshoes and bottles stuffed with needles were once found in the area.

The earliest documents found by Cudworth for Bolton Old Hall and estate were dated 1648, when the hall was owned by Richard Stanhope. It afterwards passed to John Stanhope, physician, who erected Eccleshill Hall in 1713. The estate later passed to the Barton family, who, in order to increase the income from the estate, opened up quarries in 1853. 'Pavors' from these quarries were used for the main streets of Leeds and the pavement in front of Leeds Town Hall. Consequently, Bolton Wood stone came to be in great demand and became the main stone for paving purposes. In 1862 it obtained the first prize for quality and durability for building and monumental purposes at the International Exhibition and was used for the Midland Station, the Bradford Eye and Ear Hospital, the Bradford Post Office and Manchester Town Hall. The Barton family sold the Bolton Wood estate to Messrs Constable, Holmes and Pullan, who later disposed of the land for building purposes and sold or let out quarry sites. All this activity resulted in the creation of the township of Bolton Woods.

One of the other woodland areas also used for quarrying was Cliffe Wood. A very ancient woodland site, it revealed fossil trees when the quarries were first opened. It is also said to have been the haunt of the legendary wild boar, which terrorised the town and whose tongueless head still graces the Bradford coat of arms, together with the well and a sprig from Cliffe Wood. A well, Boar's Well, was named after its drinking place there. The wood was also reputedly the burial ground of the victims of the 1665 plague. According to Joseph Fieldhouse, the infection had supposedly been conveyed from London in a bundle of old clothes. Those who became infected were taken to Cliffe Barn, adjacent to the wood, where they were left to look after one another. Food was left for them nearby. Stones found in the wood marked the graves of these victims.

Bolton House estate was also in the township of Bolton and included a portion of one of the most picturesque parks. This later became Peel Park, which was the first public park in Bradford and among the first in the country. Bolton House itself was associated with one of the oldest families of Bolton, namely the Lister family. George Thompson Lister is highlighted by Cudworth in his account. Following his failed worsted business at Redbeck Mill, Shipley Fields, Lister had to auction off Bolton House and his estate. He later became an auctioneer himself, and a land agent, and built Hollin Close as his own residence. He was quite a celebrity in his time, witty and intelligent, an excellent speaker with a large physique (nearly 30 stones) to match his personality. However, his sale of the Bolton property released his land, which led to its ultimate acquisition by the Peel Park Committee and the transfer of the parkland to the Corporation in November 1863.

Two of the main old rural settlements in Bolton are Low Fold and Hodgson Fold. Low Fold was associated with the Hustler family, well known in Bradford for their Quaker beliefs and influence and general benevolence. The family were the leading woolstaplers of Bradford. John Hustler, the first of Undercliffe, was one of the principle promoters of the Bradford Canal, which was crucial to the success of the Bolton quarries. Today Low Fold nestles behind Tetley Place at the top of Bolton Lane as a cluster of ancient cottages.

In Cudworth's time Hodgson Fold was at the centre of Bolton and consisted of a cluster of

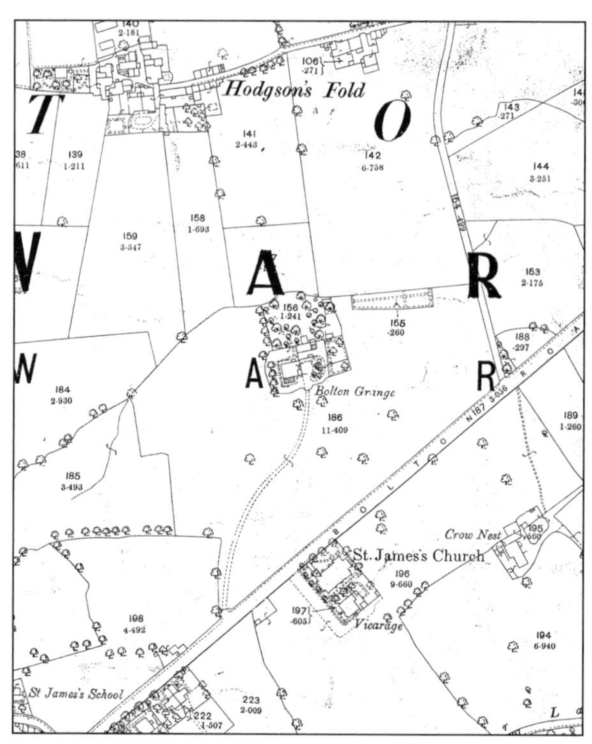


Map showing Hodgson's Fold, Bolton, *c.*1893.

A cottage in Bolton shows the importance of wool to the development of the Bradford area. *(Gina Szekely)*

A cottage in Hodgson Fold with the date 1652 and the initials of one of the Hodgson family, who owned property there for about 200 years. *(Ann Birdsall)*

old homesteads surrounded by land which was cultivated by some of the oldest yeoman families in the district. The Hodgson family was one of these and they gave the fold its name, having owned property there for around 200 years. Cudworth traces the ancestry of this family, as with others of Bolton, in the Calverley Parish registers, Bolton being part of that parish until after its own church St James's was built and opened in 1877. Today Hodgson Fold is overshadowed by the Ashbourne and Grove House Estates, just off the main Grove House Road. In 1964 the old farm there was reported to be a mink farm. One of the cottages still bears the date 1652 and the initials of one of the members of the Hodgson family. Hodgson Fold is now a conservation area.

Behind Morrison's supermarket, off Myers Lane, is Ivy Hall, built in 1616, which is known today as Bolton's oldest building. It has a large buttressed chimney with purpose-built steps on the inside which made access easy for sweeps in the past. Apparently, during the Industrial Revolution, the house was used as a hand-weaving cottage, and it is said that at one time a tunnel led from Ivy Hall to Bolling Hall. Ivy Hall once belonged to Samuel Lister of Horton, before passing to John Bailey, maltster, of Bolton. John worked the maltkiln at Hodgson Fold for nearly 30 years. Myers Lane itself was formerly known as Owl Lane, but was renamed after an old Bolton family, one of whom, Joseph Myers, cartwright, built houses there in 1788.

Perhaps the most famous, albeit temporary, resident of Bolton, was William Edward Forster, Liberal MP for Bradford, who introduced the Elementary Education Act in 1870, under the terms of which all children were to be formally educated to certain standards of literacy and numeracy, initially via board schools. Bradford's first board school was opened in Bowling Back Lane. William Cudworth notes how William Forster, when he first came to reside in the town, stayed with John Hustler, junior, at Bolton House, until he spotted Rose Cottage, where he lived comfortably for seven years as a bachelor. There he entertained relatives and many friends, including Robert Owen, the socialist, Thomas Cooper, the Chartist and Thomas Carlyle, the philosopher. He also made a philanthropic mission to Ireland during 1846. Cudworth says that he was well liked by the local children who called him 'Misser Fosser', 'Mr' being used for grand folk. He also writes of the annual 'tea-party' provided in the adjoining old maltkiln for older people, where there was a good table and afterwards entertainments, over which Forster presided. Rose Cottage was also used to stage dramatic entertainments and sometimes even a dance. When Forster left Rose Cottage in 1846, he set up home in Apperley Lane, Rawdon, and shortly afterwards married the daughter of Dr Arnold of Rugby. There is a line drawing of Rose Cottage in Cudworth's *Histories of Bolton and Bowling*.

Bolton Common was enclosed in 1819. Following its enclosure the turnpike road from Bradford to Eccleshill was begun in 1825. The toll house stood at the junction of Wapping and Bolton roads. This highway provided an outlet for the stone quarries at Cliffe Wood and Spinkwell and was therefore instrumental, just like the canal, in promoting that industry. The first property erected on the newly enclosed common in 1821 was Sefton Cottage, which during that century gained quite a reputation as the final resting place of Mrs Atkinson, who was locally renowned for fortune telling and was regularly visited by people of all classes while she lived in Horton. Apparently she grew quite rich on the proceeds and kept a bull mastiff chained at the back of her house for protection. Her life in Bolton, however, was quite secluded, and she died in her bed in 1871.

Among her possessions was a large collection of clothing, which included hundreds of fashionable dresses of many different periods, as well as a collection of herbs and nostrums.

Schooling in Bolton was started in a major way by Revd T.A. Stowell, later Canon, who first began a Sunday school, then a day school and finally a winter night school, which was attended by around 25 young men. Prior to this there is said to have been only a very small school at Bolton Common. Stowell also started a course of lectures on advanced subjects such as astronomy and chemistry. All this activity promoted the need for the National School at Bolton and this came about in 1859 with financial support from some of the leading men of the district, such as J.A. Jowett, who also built the Church of St James. Since then, Bolton has again had reason to be proud of its educational achievements, through the Lister Lane Special School.

In 1865, the time of the local board's control of Bolton, the number of homes was 320, of which 176 were below the rateable value of £5. In 1991, Bolton ward had a population of about 13,200 and was almost exclusively owner-occupied, with fewer than 450 households living in council housing. Most of the houses have been built since the 1940s. It had an unemployment rate of 6.7%, well below the district average.

**Further Reading**

**Cudworth, William** *Histories of Bolton and Bowling* Thos Brear and Co. Limited, Bradford, 1891.
**Fieldhouse, Joseph** *Bradford* Watmoughs Limited & City of Bradford MC, Libraries Division, 1981.
**Parker, James** *Illustrated Rambles from Hipperholme to Tong* Percy Lund, Humphries & Co. Ltd, The Country Press, Bradford, 1904.
**Richardson, C.** *A Geography of Bradford* University of Bradford, 1976.

Cottages in Hodgson Fold, Bolton. *(Ann Birdsall)*

Bolton Junction as it is today. *(Gina Szekely)*

Hodgson Fold in days gone by (date unknown). *(Bradford Libraries)*

The opening of the electrified Bradford tramway system, Bolton Junction, 1898. *(Bradford Libraries)*

# Bolton Woods

BOLTON Woods village grew up around the predominant local industries of coal mining, stone quarrying and textiles, which is perhaps one of the reasons that it developed in what has been described as a rather haphazard fashion. Bolton Hall Road, for example, was built in 12 separate phases, and this probably reflected the fluctuation in industry and employment in the area. According to local historian, Bill Sutcliffe, the land was also bought by three men in 1869, Messrs Constable, Holmes and Pullan, who then split the land into smaller sections and resold them as building plots to various developers, a process which contributed to the range of buildings in the area. Shann Street, begun in the 1870s, is named after one of the first of these developers. Mr Shann also built Bute Street.

Today Bolton Hall Road is relatively unchanged since 1908, but the green fields at the top of it which lay between Bolton Woods and Wrose are built upon and there is hardly any distinction between the two villages. Chestnut Grove and Primrose Lane continue as reminders of the woods which covered the nearby hill and which gave the village its name.

Stone quarrying is said to have started when two farmers replaced livestock farming with quarrying 200 years ago. In the 19th century, as many as 200 workers were employed at the quarries, almost all living in Bolton Woods. Bradford reached its peak period for stone production in the 1870s and was selling almost 450,000 tons a year, to customers as far away as Australia. Today local men still work at those quarries which remain open in the area, such as Pickards Quarry, although modern mechanisation means that far fewer men are needed to extract the carboniferous sandstone. York stone, a mellow, buff, fine-grained sandstone used for buildings or hard-wearing paving, is still in demand and is sent all over the world. Buildings for which Bolton Woods stone has been used include Elgin Cathedral, Leeds Town Hall and Bradford Grammar School. Diamond–sawn paving has been laid in market squares and pedestrian precincts, including some at Windsor Castle and Gloucester Cathedral. In 1976, Washington DC received a gift from Britain which included a stone table, designed by local workmen, to mark the American Bicentenary.

On his website, Bill Sutcliffe, whose own experiences relate to Waterhouse and Denbigh's Quarry (now Evered Natural Stone Products Ltd), writes in some detail about the hand tools that workers used and states surprisingly that quarrymen of 200 years ago would be at home with most of these used today in the smaller quarries. The differences are in the materials used to make the implements and in the mechanisation of processes to extract the stone. He also notes the local sayings which refer to changes in the weather and which were based on the necessity for relatively good weather to get any work done in the quarries. Such a phrase is 'There is nowt nobbut snow comes over from Wrose', Wrose village being to the north of the quarry and set on much higher ground, over which winter winds laden with snow came. However, quarrying has not always brought rewards to the community. Over the years, there have been a number of protests from locals regarding noise, dirt, dust and the routes of heavy lorries through Bolton Woods. In the 1970s, action groups were formed and one report tells of women and children making

Another chapel conversion. The Wesleyans built this in Stanley Road, Bolton Woods, in 1886. *(Gina Szekely)*

a human blockade across the pathway of some lorries near their houses. Fortunately, protests against planning applications for quarry expansions, which would encroach on homes, have so far been successful.

Textile employment rivalled that of quarrying in the latter part of the 1800s. Bill Sutcliffe shows figures from the 1881 census of 173 textile employees in a total of 444 workers, with only 65 employed in the quarries and stone-related jobs. This figure has increased on the 1891 census, even though at the time, the only working mill in the village was that of Bolton Woods Shed, where formerly there were three mills. Today Bolton Woods Shed, Oswin Mill and Showers Mill are still open, but Stone Bridge Mill and Frizingley Mills have been demolished.

As in most cases, the decline of the early 20th century village is marked by the reduction in the number of shops and other amenities. In the 1930s, there were 25 shops in the area, as well as a school and religious institutions, such as the Anglican church at the top end of Bolton Hall Road. Today there is no religious centre. St Laurence's Church is now in fact a private residential home. Sadly, the school was also closed during the recent school reorganisation by Bradford Local Education Authority. However, thanks to the excellent website produced by local historian Bill Sutcliffe and John Davies, school days in Bolton Woods are vividly brought to life with text and photographs. The school was opened in August 1876 and was gradually enlarged to encompass a growing population. Among some of the interesting reports of the school are the charitable collections: eggs, jams, jellies, cigarettes and postage stamps for wounded soldiers in World War One and annual egg collections for the Children's Hospital in Bradford. Educational diversions noted include National Days, introduced in around 1915, when school work was concentrated on themes such as the Battle of Trafalgar, or the culture of individual countries. The early 1920s also saw the introduction of a potential new aid to teaching – the motion picture – and Bill Sutcliffe recounts how the various schools gathered at Windsor Hall in Bradford to see *Shackleton's Expedition to the Antarctic*.

Today, like Thackley, Bolton Woods still retains a recognisable village or community spirit, largely thanks to a very active community centre and the locals who support it.

As in many areas, youth crime has been a problem, but the centre has provided a base for two very successful schemes which have tackled the problems well. Most recently youth workers set up an after-school group which has successfully worked with young people and

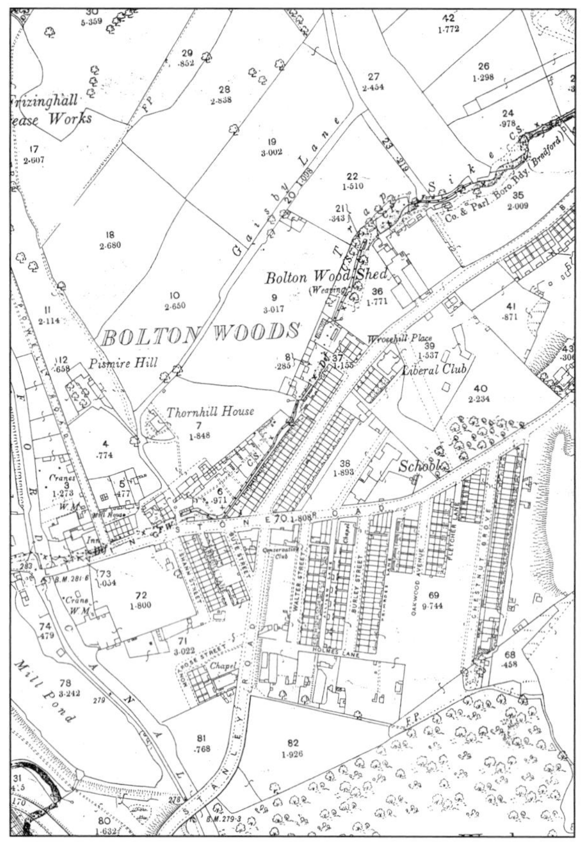


Bolton Woods shown on a map from the 1890s.

helped them secure jobs and improve their school attendance. Similarly, Bolton Woods Junior AFC, set up with just 30 youngsters in 1988, has grown into a multi-team enterprise, boasting about 400 players with 18 teams. It has attracted interest from a number of professional clubs, including Stoke, Darlington and Hull. Its website proudly announces that eight players have achieved professional status and about 20 have gone on to study sports leadership and management at college or university.

Yes, the days of Bolton Woods amateurs, with their concert parties, comic band, the carnival and fancy dress parades are gone, but despite today's hi-tech, city and club entertainments, Bolton Woods still has a public focal point for local amusement and leisure. The centre is host to weekly youth clubs, 'mums and tots' groups, pensioners' socials and a variety of educational courses, and boasts an IT learning centre. It was this which provided the impetus for the successful local history web site, which can now unite former residents from all over the world in an unprecedented way with Bolton Woods's community: past, present and future.

**Further Reading**

**Fieldhouse, Joseph** *Bradford* Watmoughs Limited & City of Bradford MC, Libraries Division, 1981.

**Richardson, C.** *A Geography of Bradford* University of Bradford, 1976.

Bolton Woods Community Centre, which has already stimulated so much unity and local achievement. *(Gina Szekely)*

Bolton Hall Road, little changed since 1908, and the scene of a human blockade against quarry traffic in 1976. *(Gina Szekely)*

Oswin Mills, Bolton Woods, latterly used by Diamond Seal double-glazing company. *(Bradford Libraries)*

# BOWLING

BOWLING lies to the south of the city of Bradford, close to the city centre, and as anyone familiar with the districts that make up the city will know, it comprises East and West Bowling, separate communities with their own identities. This chapter aims to describe the ancient history of Bowling as a whole, before looking at the modern history and current state of the township.

Bowling takes its name from the early English word *bolle* (pronounced 'bowl') meaning 'bull', and *ing*, which means field, so Bowling is literally 'field of the bull'. The manor of Bollinc, the Domesday Book tells us, was where Sindi had four carucates of land. Furthermore, Domesday tells us that 'Ilbert has it and it is waste'. Ilbert was Ilbert de Lacy, who had much of west Yorkshire handed to him by William the Conqueror.

Bowling is referred to in the records relating to Richard II's infamous poll tax of 1379. This list tells us that 20 people in the township of 'Bollyng' were liable for taxation, the largest amount being owed by Johannes de Bollyng Esquire. Other names famous in Bradford's history appear on the list, notably the Heatons (given as Heton), the Illingworths (Ellynworth) and the Fieldhouses. The Bolling family were linked with Bowling from as early as the reign of King John (1199–1216) when Tristram Bolling received property in the area in return for his services to the king. The Bolling family were to hold on to the manor for several centuries, vastly increasing its size in 1349 when Thornton, Allerton and Denholme were added following the marriage of Robert Bolling and Elizabeth Thornton. The manor was lost to the Bollings for a time when Robert Bolling (another one!) sided with the Lancastrians at the battle of Towton (1461), and following defeat was convicted of high treason, his estate being confiscated. The estates were eventually recovered and passed into the hands of the Tempest family, another name synonymous with the history of the Bradford district. Bolling Hall, the long-time seat of the Bolling, Tempest and Lindley Wood families, still exists as a fine museum, one of Bradford's oldest and most impressive former manor houses. It was a family home for more than five centuries and it is easy to see why, with its stunning views right over the city towards the open hills and moors. Today the hall is furnished to give an idea of what it would have been like to live there at various times during its history. And, of course, the hall is home to Bradford's most famous ghost.

One of the bedrooms at Bolling Hall is generally known as the Ghost Room. Nobody within living memory has actually seen a ghost there, but there is a story that one appeared there once, long ago.

The Civil War raged up and down the country during the 1640s. Bradford's first association with the conflict was in December 1642. The town was very Puritan, the local people valuing their right to read and discuss the Bible as they chose, to worship as they liked, and to listen to their own choice of preachers. The town, therefore, was generally sympathetic to Oliver Cromwell, and his idea that Parliament, not the king alone, should have the final say in all matters of law. Bolling Hall then stood outside Bradford, with a commanding view over the town towards the parish church and the main streets of Ivegate and Kirkgate. The owner, Sir Richard Tempest, belonged to the old school who believed that the king alone had the right, received directly from God, to rule as he saw fit, and that Parliament should be lower. He was a Royalist.

The town of Bradford was besieged by the Royalist army, under the Earl of Newcastle, in December 1642. The Earl of Newcastle stayed with Sir Richard Tempest at Bolling Hall, and looked down on this small town from the hill above it. Bradford held out strongly, in spite of having no army and no fortifications, and the Earl was naturally annoyed. The story tells that he was very cross, one Sunday evening, at Bradford's continued resistance and, as he went to bed, declared that the following morning he would slaughter every man, woman and child in the place, in spite of this being against the general code of conduct for war. He then went to sleep. During the night the Earl was awakened by feeling the bedclothes being pulled off him. By his bed stood a ghost, wringing its hands and saying, 'Pity poor Bradford!' The Earl was suitably shaken and, the following morning, said that he had changed his mind. He would still attack Bradford, but would now only slaughter those who offered real armed resistance. Bradford was duly attacked, and taken by the Royalists. There were very few casualties, probably less than 10, who died of wounds received in the skirmishing. So the people of Bradford could have been saved by this mysterious apparition!

Bowling was the birthplace of the infamous prophet John Wroe. He was born on 19 September 1782 at Rooley Lane. Wroe went through an unhappy period in his life and also suffered an illness which made him temporarily blind. He turned to religion and became a follower of George Turner, who was the leader of the Yorkshire followers of Joanna Southcott, who declared she would give birth to a Messiah. Wroe succeeded Turner as the leader of the Christian Israelites, as they called themselves. He had a mission to preach to all nations. He did so in many European countries. Apparently he had the power to heal and rid folk of demons. He had thousands of followers who believed he had supernatural powers. Over 30,000 people flocked to Apperley Bridge to see him perform a miracle.

Industry on a large scale came relatively early to Bowling with the opening of Bowling Ironworks in the early 1780s. The original workings were on Jeremiah Rawson's estate, near Lower Lane, extending in time onto the estate of Mr Francis Lindley Wood in West Bowling. Bowling was lucky in that it lies on beds of both black bed ironstone and a better bed of coal, both quite near to the surface and easily extracted. Iron from the Bowling works was to become well known worldwide. The industry thrived, and similar works were opened on the same mineral beds in Low Moor and Bierley. Housing and facilities for the workers began to spring up across Bowling, and the township flourished.

For many years Bowling township was bereft of anything resembling a proper, structured system of local government. Leading members of the community met in the Wheat Sheaf Inn for 30 years after 1770, and a study of the records and accounts is available in *Histories of Bolton and Bowling* by William Cudworth. The Charter of Incorporation granted to Bradford in 1847 led to Bowling joining with other townships such as Manningham, Horton and of course Bradford itself to form the new Borough of Bradford. Bowling had its own representatives to sit on the new council, and had a Burgess Roll (or early Electoral Roll) comprising 715 voters. In 1882 Bowling was split into two council wards – East and West Bowling. By this time the Burgess Roll for the two wards had a combined total of 5,847, an increase of over five thousand in just 35 years. Bradford was increasing rapidly, and Bowling was being swept along on the tide. Indeed, the total population of Bowling at this time was

Bowling Iron Company's Works, *c.*1861.

John Wroe's birthplace, Bowling. *(Bradford Libraries)*

almost 29,000, compared to just over 2,000 at the turn of the 19th century.

Apart from the ironworks, Bowling's other industries included dyeing – Ripley's dye works was a well-established Bowling company, and, like much of the Bradford district, the worsted trade was prevalent. Victoria Mill on Wakefield Road, Lady Well Mill (Hall Lane) and Upper Croft Mill were but three of the many worsted operations in the area. One of the leading businessmen in the Bowling area was Henry Ripley (later Sir Henry, Bart.) owner of the previously mentioned dye works. He built around 200 houses for his workforce in the early 1860s, intending them to pay a little extra on the rent in order to slowly buy the properties for themselves. The project (called Ripleyville) was ultimately unsuccessful as few of the workforce chose to make the extra payments. Mr Ripley also provided schools and the land on which St Bartholomew's Church was built. Ripley Street still exists, bearing the name of a man who, like Sir Titus Salt, sought to bring about the betterment of those he employed.

So Bowling has a long history as a separate, independent township, with its leading families, its own industries and a community proud to be Bowlingites. The 20th century was to bring many changes to the city as a whole, and Bowling certainly did not escape. Today it is unrecognisable from the Bowling of yesteryear.

The ward covers 2.3 square miles and has a large population of 17,800. The area contains a mixture of industry and housing. Much of the industry is concentrated in the Broomfields area, between the Manchester and Wakefield Roads. Much of this area used to be housing but large amounts were cleared to make way for new roads and industry. East Bowling roughly covers the area bordered by Wakefield Road and Rooley Lane, whereas West Bowling joins onto East Bowling and runs to Manchester Road.

Manchester Road is one of the busiest routes in and out of the city centre, and it splits West Bowling from Little Horton. The road is actually quite unique, having something in common with only three other cities; Essen, Adelaide and Leeds! It is one of the few places to provide a guided bus scheme. This runs from Jacobs Well in the city centre, up to Netherlands Avenue in Low Moor. Buses can now travel up and down Manchester Road in a separate, guided lane, right in the middle of the carriageway. The buses get priority at traffic lights by means of a special loop in the track which recognises when they are approaching. This in effect means that the buses can travel the whole length of Manchester Road without getting caught in any traffic. The scheme opened in March 2002 and included the installation of new pedestrian crossings and bus shelters. The shelters themselves are quite unique in the fact that they are heated in winter by their own wind turbines and they even play music to suit your mood while you wait for a bus. Twenty-first century travel has certainly arrived in this part of Bradford.

The new guided buses would have come in handy for some at the start of the 20th century. This was when the Manchester Road pub crawl was at its peak. There were around 60 public houses situated on the street. By the 1930s the number had decreased to around 30, but the crawl is still a popular talking point today. Many people started at the Majestic, near the city centre, and made their way up to Odsal Top. Then it was back down to the city centre on the other side of the street. Not a night out for the faint-hearted!

East Bowling has recently arrived on the 'pop-music map'. Local lad Gareth Gates, a pupil at Dixons City Technology College in West Bowling, entered the 'Pop Idol' competition on television, and nearly went all the way. He eventually finished as runner up,

Manchester Road, 1976. Bordering Bowling, this was the home of the infamous Manchester Road pub-crawl. *(Jack Booth)*

The 'haunted' Bolling Hall. *(Bradford Libraries)*

but by the final show he had already become a superstar. His first single went straight in at number one and he is destined to be a huge star, at the tender age of 17. Girls and women of all ages fell for his youthful good looks and wonderful vocals. Let's hope that all the fame does not make Gareth forget his roots and his hometown. He has certainly put Bowling and Bradford on the map for the right reasons.

**Further Reading**

**Cudworth, W.** *Histories of Bolton and Bowling* Thomas Brear and Co., 1891.

Sir Henry Ripley, builder of Ripleyville, owner of Bowling dye works and MP between 1874 and 1880. *(Bradford Libraries)*

Bolling Hall pictured in 1969. *(Bradford Libraries)*

New Hey Road cricket team show off their medals. The picture dates from the 1930s. *(Bradford Libraries)*

Bowling Back Lane open-air school, pictured in 1917. *(Bradford Libraries)*

# Bradford Moor

EXACTLY where Bradford Moor begins and ends has caused much debate over the years. Its boundary with Thornbury seems to have been equally controversial. John Stanley King in a *Telegraph & Argus* article of December 1968 defined Bradford Moor as originally being 'the common or waste moorland attached to the original township of Bradford, and the last remnant of common land there was finally enclosed just over a century ago.' He further defined the boundary with Thornbury as being approximately where Bradford Moor Park and Crofts works stood. The modern boundary of the city of Bradford is at Gain Lane, and between these two boundaries lies Thornbury, part of Calverley until 1 May 1882 when Bradford took control of it. A *T & A* article of September 1987 claimed that if you were to ask anyone living in Bradford Moor where it starts and ends you would be met with an uncertain reply, half of the population believing that they live in Thornbury, while others think they are in Laisterdyke! Surely this is not quite the case, but some confusion does seem to exist.

The council ward of Bradford Moor is much more easily identified than the ill-defined district that shares its name, its borders being clearly set out by Bradford Council in its Ward Profile. It is the city's smallest ward, covering a mere half square mile of mainly built up areas at the top end of Leeds Road, bordering the open country between Bradford and Leeds. It contains three council estates – Bradford Moor estate, Napier Street and Thornbury estate.

The early recorded history of Bradford Moor seems to be riddled with tales of disagreement and dispute. The Moors lay on high land to the east of Bradford, and the neighbouring manors of Calverley and Bradford both believed that they held the right of pasture and turbary (the digging of turves). As early as the 1400s Bradford Moor is mentioned in the Bradford Court Rolls, in relation to pasturing offences, and the illegal movement of carts of ironstone. On one occasion a significant number of men from Calverley were accused of digging turves on the moor without permission. Parts of the moor were mapped in around 1720 as a direct result of a dispute between Sir Walter Calverley and a Mr Marsden, then lord of the manor of Bradford. The map aimed to set out the boundaries of the area, and a study of the map, the dispute and the boundaries appeared in the *Bradford Antiquary* in 1985.

Bradford Moor was lucky enough (or perhaps unlucky enough) to be situated on a seam of coal some 18in thick. As the use of coal increased with the dawning of the industrial age, so the number of mines and collieries across the Bradford district increased. Bradford Moor became one of the more developed mining areas within the town. Some sites were worked for many years, including Bunkers Hill Colliery, which stretched across Myrashay and up both sides of Barkerend Road. The colliery was probably named after the Battle of Bunkers Hill in America in 1775, although it was already in existence under an unknown name well before this date.

Bradford Moor was crossed by the Dudley Hill to Killinghall Turnpike, built on an old track shown on maps as the road to Eccleshill. Two toll bars were erected in Bradford Moor, one at the crossroads of Killinghall and Fagley Roads, the other between Laisterdyke and Bowling Back Lane. Toll bars were deeply unpopular with the masses however, and

Cottage dated 1786, Silverhill Road, Bradford Moor. *(Ann Birdsall)*

Bradford Moor Park. The lake is on the site of the 'grandstand' used for the infamous horse races. *(Gina Szekely)*

damage was reported to both. More trouble involving the inhabitants of Bradford Moor occurred in 1826 when 200 men from the area joined 250 from Fairweather Green in attacking Horsfall's Mill at nearby North Wing. The mill had recently been equipped with power looms, unleashing the wrath of the local workforce who saw such mechanisation as a direct threat to their livelihoods. The mill was attacked twice within the space of a few days. On the first occasion the Riot Act was read and the damage done was limited to a few broken windows. During the second incident, however, shots were fired by the 40 men defending the mill, leaving 18-year-old Jonas Bairstow and 13-year-old Edward Fearnley lying dead. Several others were injured and two men were arrested and sent to York Castle for their part in the disturbances. Such protests were, ultimately, futile. Bradford Moor got its own mills – William Pearson's mill had been built in 1815, Bradford Moor Mills followed in 1845, while Fifth Mill was erected in nearby Laisterdyke.

Bradford Moor was expanding, along with most other parts of Bradford, at this time. The rise of Bradford's worsted trade led to the town growing at an alarming rate, as mill after mill was built and people flooded into the area in search of work. Rows and rows of houses were erected up and around Leeds Road, which had recently been extended, joining Green Lane, Leeds Old Road and Dick Lane at nearby Thornbury. Older houses pre-dating the industrialisation of Bradford still exist in Bradford Moor. One such stands on Silver Hill Road and is dated 1786. This is thought to be the last place in Bradford Moor where cloth was hand woven.

Up until 1877 the moor was the site of the notorious Bradford Moor Races – an annual event that would have had the Jockey Club throwing up its collective hands in horror. There were usually three races, featuring horses more used to pulling coal carts or milk floats than carrying jockeys, leading to some very fractious, ill-tempered beasts taking part. Huge crowds would gather for the spectacle, the surrounding streets being almost clogged up with stalls of all descriptions. The last time the races were held (1877) was a typically bloody affair and led to the council banning future events. The spectators, some of whom were assembled on the course grandstand (actually a large heap of dirt) saw Chancellor, owned by Mr Scrivener, take the overall winner's prize of a trophy and 10 pounds. Mr Bowsers' Adventurer meanwhile got rid of his jockey during the first race, leaving the unfortunate lad with a badly twisted neck. Adventurer was eventually recaptured, but not before he'd knocked spectators over left, right and centre. The injuries continued apace throughout the day and on into the evening as drunken spectators brawled their way homewards. The whole spectacle was too much for Bradford Council, who purchased the land used for the races from Miss Rawson for the princely sum of £8,768. The council soon opened Bradford Moor Park on the site, complete with a lake where the 'grandstand' had stood, and it has been enjoyed by locals, glad of such a large open space in their midst, ever since. Racing on Bradford Moor was, happily, a thing of the past!

Bradford Moor was the site of an army barracks between 1884 and the early 1930s. The Green Howards, the 70th West Riding Brigade Royal Artillery and the Royal Army Service Corps were all based there at one time or another. The last remaining link to the barracks – the Barrack Tavern at the junction of Killinghall and Leeds Old Roads – was recently turned into an Asian restaurant.

Bradford Moor Golf Club was opened in 1906 on roughly 70 acres of farmland to the west of Killinghall Road. It quickly established a reputation for producing quality players, and between the wars its members took every honour in county golf. Joe Gent, the club's most prominent player of the era, went on to become one of the country's best amateur players. Bradford Moor has another claim to sporting fame, for it was once home to Joe Johnson, 1986 World Snooker Champion. The

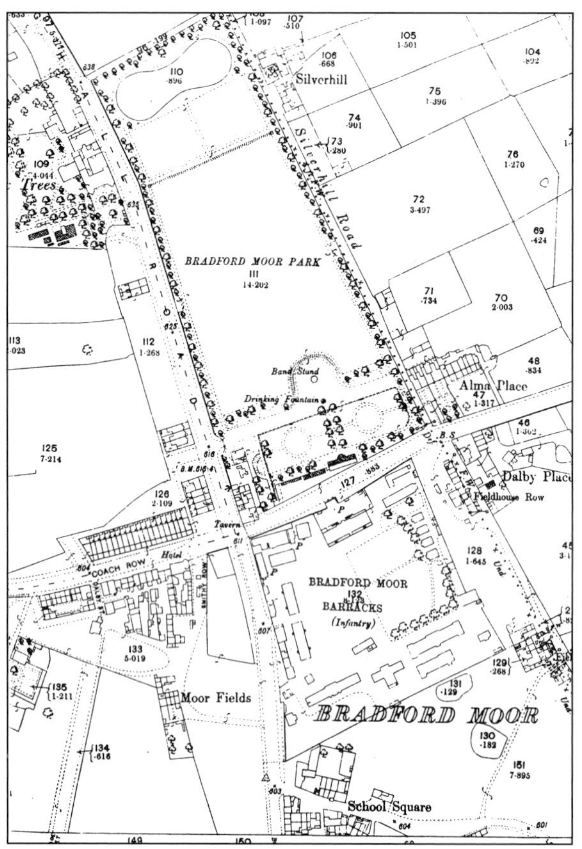


Bradford Moor park and barracks, shown on a map from the 1890s.

former gas fitter, a 150/1 outsider, won a thrilling final against Steve Davis, then regarded as the best player in the game. The match finished 18-12, and the press dubbed Johnson the 'Champion from nowhere'. Johnson replied that he wasn't from nowhere – he was from Bradford, and proud of it.

Today, despite being a substantially developed and built up suburb of Bradford, Bradford Moor retains some cherished open spaces. The park and golf club still thrive and are popular, although the threat of development on the golf course never seems far away. For now, though, both provide much needed greenery among the rows of houses and shops. Bradford Moor is not without its troubles, and the housing estate which bears its name has recently been the centre of local press attention following a spate of vandalism and accusations of verbal abuse and intimidation by groups of youngsters. As recently as March 2002 two ward councillors called for a curfew to be imposed on troublemakers to keep them off the streets and help ease residents' fears. The police were keen to try all other methods available to them before applying for such an order.

In the 1991 census, Bradford Moor ward had a population of about 16,400, over half of which consisted of ethnic minorities, mainly Pakistani and Indian in origin. The ward also had the highest proportion of children in the district – 33.1 percent being under 16. Bradford Moor has many of the usual facilities of urban life – varied shops and businesses, schools, places of worship, and a community centre on Upper Rushton Road. Bradford Moor's history is all around – the park, the late 18th and early to mid-19th century housing and the debate about where its boundaries lie, which still rumbles on some 500 years after that court case. One would be hard pressed, however, to find many reminders of the moor that gave it its name.

**Further Reading**

**Bradford Moor Retired Mens Forum** *A History of Bradford Moor.*

Bradford Moor was the site of an army barracks until the early 1930s. *(Bradford Libraries)*

Bowling Green at Bradford Moor Park. The perfect way to spend a Sunday afternoon! *(Bradford Libraries)*

The park was opened in 1878 after Bradford Council purchased the land, which was used for the notorious races, from Miss Rawson for the princely sum of £8,768. *(Bradford Libraries)*

# BUTTERSHAW

BUTTERSHAW is in the south of the city, adjoining the village of Wibsey. Its population today is 9,872. Buttershaw today is known merely as a huge post-war council estate. This is a far cry from the moorland that used to cover the area. According to Cudworth, Buttershaw's name has Saxon origins. Literally it means 'in my cottage near a wood'. 'Shaw' can be translated as 'a wood', while 'Butter' is a corruption of the Anglo-Saxon *botyl*, a dwelling. This comes from the verb *bytlian*, to build.

Despite its Anglo-Saxon name, the original village of Buttershaw was quite a modern creation. It only began to grow after the large worsted mill owned by S. Bottomley and Brothers was built on Buttershaw Roughs. Before the mill was built, the 'Roughs' were rugged moorland, hence the name. The whole area was in a 'rough' state. It was land covered in gorse and boulders. It was not until the boulders were cut up for building materials that the land became clear and ploughable, suitable for farming.

The Bottomley Bros. (Samuel, Thomas and James), who originated from Shelf, built the mills and manufacturing started in 1852. They began their business at Brighouse, and also had a mill at Low Moor. Alongside the factory significant workers' housing sprang up. Much of this still exists around Fleece Street and Bottomley Street, just off the Halifax Road. However, Buttershaw is famed for another type of housing.

Buttershaw estate was built in the 1950s to house residents from the old back-to-back terraced houses near the centre of Bradford, which were then being demolished. The main body of the estate is situated between Wibsey Park Avenue and Beacon Road, the 'official' centre being Ridings Way. When the estate was built it did not consist of soulless flats or high-rise blocks. It was mainly smaller flats, terraced and semi-detatched houses, many with gardens. However, with hindsight, one can now see the social problems which resulted from locating the estate in such an isolated area. Combined with the location, mass unemployment helped exacerbate the estate's problems. The problems reached their peak in the mid-1990s when the estate became known as the cheapest place in West Yorkshire to buy drugs, and unfortunately there were all too many takers. The estate had hit a low, but it is now back on the road to recovery. Millions of pounds have been spent on regeneration. The heart of the estate, the Boulevard, was once branded as being worse than the Gorbals in Glasgow. However, this whole area has now been revamped and even renamed. The once infamous street is now known as Ridings Way. Flats and houses have been renovated or demolished to be replaced by new accommodation. A millennium green has been created to provide a green haven on the estate. Hopefully the money now being spent will mean that the estate has a brighter future.

Buttershaw gained national fame in the 1980s with the release of the film *Rita Sue and Bob Too*, by local writer Andrea Dunbar. She had grown up on the estate but shocked her neighbours and friends with her warts and all portrayal of Buttershaw life. *Rita Sue and Bob Too* was originally penned as a play, but it was only after it was made into a film and released on television and video that her tale of under-age sex, violence, alcoholism and racism hit home. Many locals still complain that the film was unfair. They said the film stereotyped the

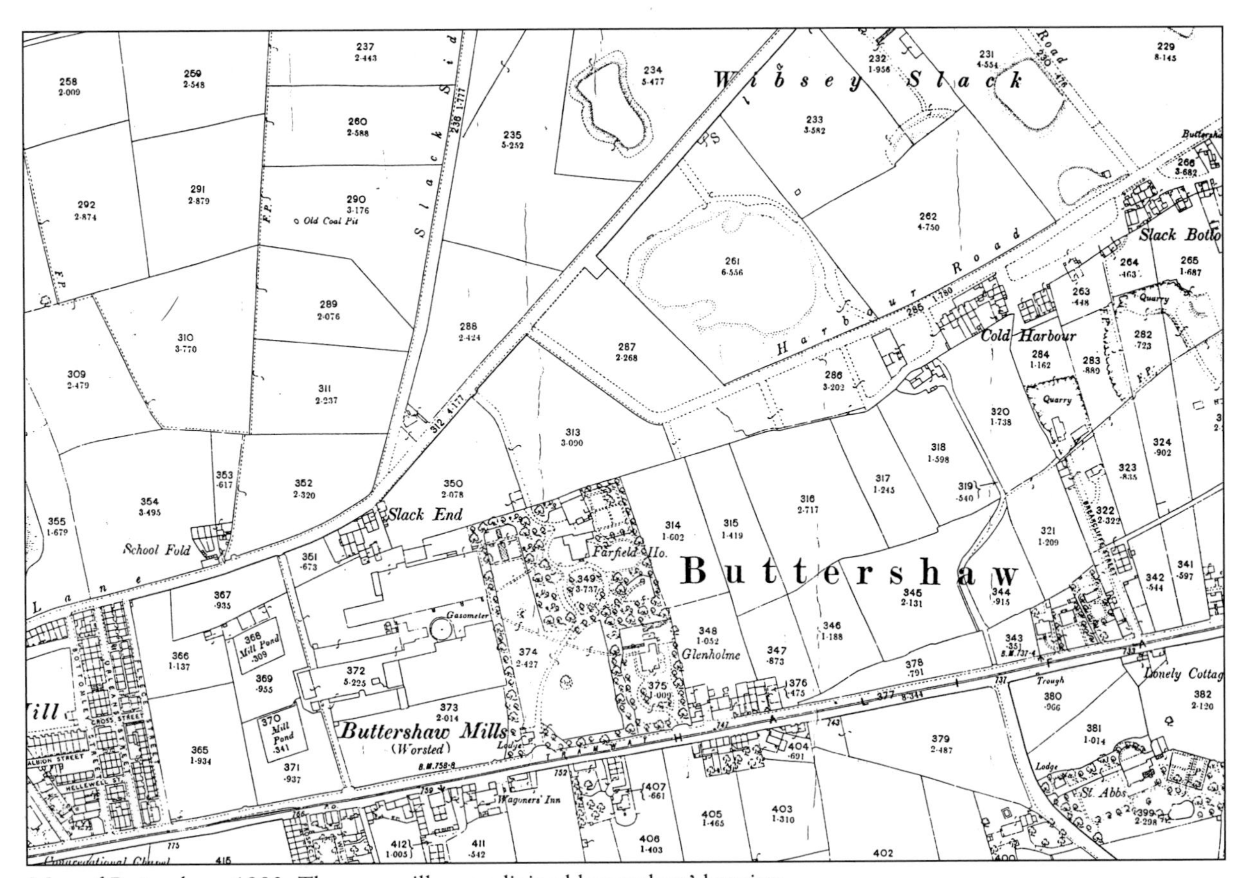

Map of Buttershaw, 1893. The new mills are adjoined by workers' housing.

Buttershaw Mills, 2002. The mills are now home to a fitness centre. *(Pete Walker)*

people of Buttershaw and were angry that they had been portrayed in such a light. Others pointed out that the filming took place in areas where housing had been earmarked for redevelopment. Indeed, many of the houses were actually empty when filming took place.

There were others on the estate, however, that were proud of Andrea Dunbar's achievement. A 'local girl made good'! Unfortunately Dunbar did not live long enough to appreciate her own success. She tragically collapsed and died in her local pub in 1990, suffering from a brain haemmorrhage at the age of 29. She would certainly be proud to see what is happening on the estate today. The Royds Project, of which Buttershaw is part, has helped pump over £20 million into the area. Buttershaw was home to the first Healthy Living Centre in the country. It now provides comfortable accommodation for older people. There is an award-winning secondary school, a huge increase in child literacy, programmes to help drug users and education for potential users. There was even a programme to plant over 2,000 trees in the area, as well as providing the millennium green. All in all, it is an estate with a bright future. An estate which will make people from Buttershaw proud again.

**Further Reading**

**Cudworth, W.** *Round About Bradford* Thomas Brear and Co., 1876.

One of the new 'gateways' to the Buttershaw Estate, 2002. *(Pete Walker)*

Buttershaw High School, 2002. This was one of the locations for the film *Rita Sue and Bob Too*. *(Pete Walker)*

# Clayton

CLAYTON was an ancient settlement and was mentioned in the Domesday Book. It was part of the Manor of Bolton, under the control of Ilbert de Lacy. At that time it was known as 'Claitone', meaning 'clay soil'. When Clayton ceased to be part of the Manor of Bolton, it was split into three parts; Clayton Village, Clayton Heights and Cockan, a now non-existent village which lay to the south-west of the present village.

Between 1160 and 1316, Clayton belonged to a gentleman named Hugh Stapleton. It then passed through several hands until it was acquired by the Bollings in 1324. The Bolling family, and their successors the Tempests, held the Manor of Clayton for nearly 300 years, until it descended to the Lacies of Cromwell-bottom by marriage. After the Lacies sold the manor in around 1740, it passed through many hands until 1894, when the district council was formed. The council fought off an attempt by Bradford Corporation in 1898 to amalgamate Clayton with the city of Bradford, and for many years the villagers enjoyed their independence. Inevitably though, in 1930, Clayton finally became part of the city of Bradford, much to the reluctance of many of the residents.

Up until the end of the 19th century, Clayton was almost all green land with very few buildings indeed. Looking at maps from 1893, it was only a very small village surrounded by fields. In the early 20th century much development took place but the village still had its green belt surrounding it. Even today, Clayton is separated from its nearest neighbours by fields. It must be a ramblers' paradise. One can walk to Thornton, Queensbury and even Ogden reservoir through the fields and across moors.

Prior to 1878, when the railway station opened, the only means of transport to and from the village would have been by foot or horse. The station was on the Bradford, Halifax and Keighley branch of the Great Northern Railway, and was situated on Pasture Lane. This meant that it was only 12 minutes to Bradford via rail and only 23 minutes to Halifax. Quicker than today, it seems. The branch line closed in 1955 and the entrance to the Queensbury tunnel was blocked and sealed up. The railway might have made it easier for residents to leave the village, but there was actually not much need for this. Clayton was quite self-sufficient. Many shops had opened in the Clayton Lane area. In 1900 there was a draper, grocers, newsagent, shoe maker, beer retailer, butcher, milliner, confectioner, builder and even a clogger. What more could the residents wish for? This was then the heart of the village. Several pubs also served the area. There was the Whittle and Steel, the Crown and the Sportsman. Some of those pubs still exist today, such as the Albion, with its wonderful collection of pictures of Old Clayton, and the Black Bull.

During the 20th century, much residential development took place in the area, although the 'village' feel was retained. Clayton is not simply another sprawling suburb of Bradford. It seems to retain some sort of independence. This individuality attracts people from all over Bradford to live within Clayton's boundaries. Today there are still a number of shops and businesses in the village, most of them family-owned.

One of the focal points of today's village is Victoria Park. The park actually originates from the old village green. In 1897, a meeting of

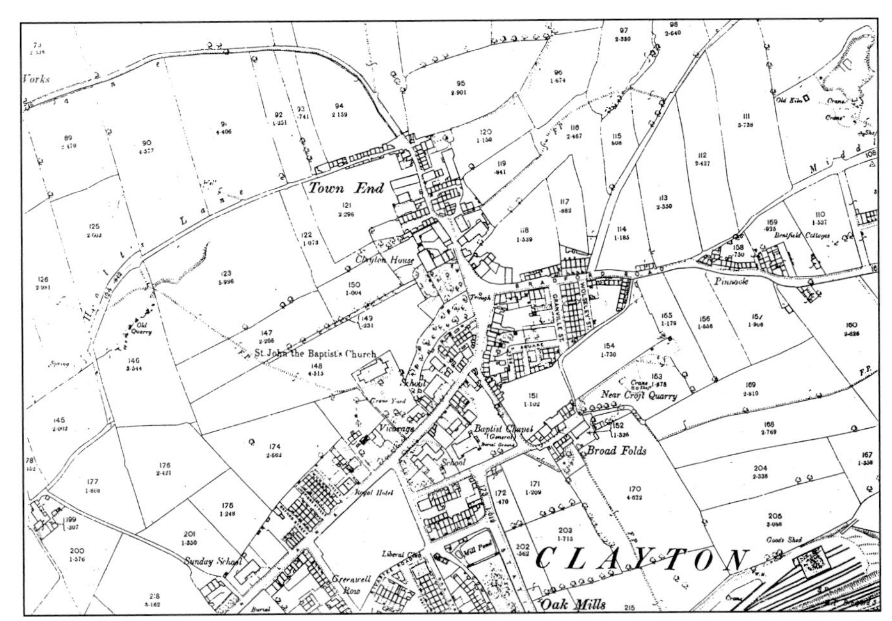


Map of Clayton, 1893. Note the troughs or wells in the centre of the village, and the railway to the south-east.

residents was held at which it was proposed that the village green and surrounding land be purchased to form a park. It was suggested that the park be created for the use of Clayton residents for ever, and donations were collected so that the project could succeed without any cost to the ratepayers, although the park's upkeep would be paid for by the rates. The scheme was started in commemoration of the Diamond Jubilee of Queen Victoria and the park finally opened on 23 July 1898. It was opened by Asa Briggs, the highly respected Claytonian philanthropist.

The roundabout in Clayton is home to the 'wells'. The wells were stone troughs which

Clayton, *c.*1900. Horses taking refreshment at the 'wells'. *(Bradford Libraries)*

supplied water in days gone by. Householders without water supply would bring their own buckets here to fill up, and carters on their way to Queensbury or Thornton would stop here to let their horses drink. The area was a popular meeting place in times past.

One of Clayton's biggest claims to fame is that it was the birthplace and home of Albert Pierrepoint, Britain's last 'Number One' official hangman. In his role as state executioner Pierrepoint despatched some of the country's most notorious convicted murderers – while expressing some personal reservations about the value and use of capital punishment.

Alfred Wallis was a well-known and respected Claytonian. He started business in Oak Mills in 1860, with Asa Briggs and Joseph Benn. He was active in Clayton's affairs for many years and he set up the Alfred Wallis Trust Fund, which can still be used today for the further education of Clayton's young people.

Another of the area's characters was known as the 'Clayton poet'. Sherwin Stephenson was born in the village in 1881. He became a talented poet, describing his experiences and life in Clayton. He penned such verses as; 'Bonny Clayton', 'Teah Pot Spaht', 'The Old Brewery, Clayton', 'Cote Fields' and 'My Native Hills', all celebrating the people and surroundings of Clayton. He even described the wells as a meeting place of the 'Clayton Parliament'. A true ambassador for the village, Sherwin died in 1954. He is buried in Clayton churchyard, where his headstone resembles an open book.

Stephenson's poems are a perfect reminder of how Clayton used to be. The village will never be the same again, but it is one of the few areas of Bradford which has retained its character somewhat. Stephenson would be proud.

**Further Reading**

**Cudworth, W.** *Round About Bradford* Thomas Brear and Co., 1876.
**Dalgety, M.** *Clayton: Then and Now* Countryside Publications, 1985.

The wells today. You do not see horses here nowadays, unless you watch them in the nearby bookies. *(Pete Walker)*

The grand opening of Victoria Park, 1898. *(Bradford Libraries)*

Town End, Clayton, 2002. *(Pete Walker)*

Ox-roasting at Clayton to celebrate the distribution of lodge funds from the Working Men's Club. *(Bradford Libraries)*

Annual tea for the employees of Asa Briggs, *c.*1910. *(Bradford Libraries)*

Clayton Silver Prize Band, photographed in the Greenside Lane garden of Asa Briggs, who is standing in the doorway. The band had just won a prize at Crystal Palace. *(Bradford Libraries)*

# DUDLEY HILL

THE origins of the area of Bradford known as Dudley Hill offer several possibilities. William Cudworth found an explanation in the Norse *doed-lande*, meaning barren or dead land, and justified this theory by stating that 'dead land is not a bad description of much of the soil in this locality as it was some fifty or sixty years ago,' (he was writing in 1876). The reference work *Place names of the West Riding* finds Dudley Hill first used as a place name in 1715 and gives the probable explanation as 'Dudde's Clearing'.

The name seems to have first been applied to the area immediately surrounding the crossroads of Wakefield Road and the Wibsey to Leeds Road. The community that sprang up here owed its existence to the early years of the Industrial Revolution. Improved communication and transport links were essential at this time, and the Dudley Hill area had three turnpike roads pass through it, namely the Leeds, Bradford and Halifax Road (opened 1740), the Bradford to Wakefield Road (1752) and the Killinghall and Harrogate Road (also 1752). The opening of the nearby Bowling Ironworks in the 1780s was also instrumental in the growth of Dudley Hill, both in terms of population, as people moved in to the area having gained employment in the works' mining and smelting operations, and physically, as houses were built to accommodate them.

In his 1891 work *Histories of Bolton and Bowling* Cudworth tells us that card-setting was the main local trade in the early 19th century, and as this task was carried out by hand, back then, mainly by women and children, it must have been a common sight in the summer months to see the womenfolk sat outside their cottages toiling over their labours. The introduction of the factory system was to change people's working practices, and indeed their whole lives, forever. The first mill in Dudley Hill, called Terry's Mill, went up on Sticker Lane in 1833. The 1842 'plug-drawing riots' saw local workers, angry at what they saw as the end of their traditional working ways, and fearful of the increasing number of factories and mills being built, attempt to let off the water from the boilers at Terry's Mill. A troop of cavalry had to be sent from Leeds to disperse the angry mob. The riots were in vain, of course, as industrialisation marched on, seemingly unchecked. Many more mills went up in the Dudley Hill area in the period 1850 to 1890, including Albion Mills, Scott's and Hillas's. Dudley Hill was fortunate enough to have its own railway station, opened in 1856, always a sign of a district's expansion and growing importance.

By the turn of the century many fine amenities had been provided for the vastly increased population of the Dudley Hill area. A telegraph office had been opened in 1881, and the nearby Bowling Park, Bowling Baths and library were all readily available for public recreation, as were the many pubs that had sprung up in the area. The residents' more spiritual needs were amply catered for as well, with well-established places of worship, such as the Wesleyan Chapel and the Ebenezer Primitive Methodist, both of which were opened in 1823. The congregations that built these chapels had emerged from the classes formed a few generations earlier, following a visit to the area, in 1744, by the preacher John Wesley.

Dudley Hill plays its part in one of Bradford's stranger religious tales, for it was from there that the prophet John Wroe regularly led a procession of 12 women, whom he described as his '12 virgins'. John Wroe was a Bowlingite by birth, and was baptised at Bradford parish church in 1782. Shortly after his marriage he was struck down by a powerful fever from which he made a slow recovery. From this point on, however, he began to 'see visions and to dream dreams', and would lie for hours in a trance-like state when 'angels' appeared to him telling of events that were to happen to him. He eventually became the leader of a sect of Southcottians (who followed the prophecies of Joanna Southcott) and many Bradfordians would flock to hear him preach and prophesise on Sunday afternoons, at services he held in the old Cockpit building. It must have been a sight to see, in Dudley Hill, as his procession set off for Bradford, his 'virgins' walking in single file each clothed all in white and wearing veils of the same colour. A television drama of *Mr Wroe's Virgins* was recently made, proving that such interesting characters live long in the collective memory.

In 1912 Dudley Hill became one of the first areas in West Yorkshire to boast a cinema, with the opening of the Picture Palace, known locally as 't' Dud'. Visitors to t' Dud were fortunate indeed, for the cinema was the first in the city to install a thermostatically controlled oil-fired boiler. Luxury indeed! The cinema, like most suburban ones, eventually fell on hard times, showing its last film in 1967. The red-brick building, with its grand façade, was used as a bingo hall before becoming a carpet warehouse.

Dudley Hill was home to one of Bradford's two greyhound tracks. The Greenfield Stadium was opened in 1927 and regularly attracted throngs of hopeful punters looking to make their fortunes. Like many a punter's dreams, however, the track eventually 'went to the dogs', closing for racing in 1969.

The 1950s and 1960s saw massive changes to the physical appearance of Dudley Hill with the demolition of many fine old buildings to facilitate various road widening and 'improvement' schemes. It is fair to assume that someone living in the Dudley Hill of the early 1950s would have felt quite at home with the appearance of the place if they were transported back in time to the turn of the century, and would even recognise the names of some of the shops and businesses in the area. It is equally fair to say that someone growing up in modern Dudley Hill would struggle to recognize much of their surroundings if they were taken back to the early 1950s, such is the scale of the changes.

The road-widening schemes were inevitable given the vastly increased levels of traffic, and perhaps Dudley Hill suffered more than other areas within the city, leading to road safety issues dominating the minds of many local residents. There was widespread approval and relief when a pelican crossing was finally installed on busy Sticker Lane in 1996. Despite the roads which threatened to physically split and divide the community, the strong community spirit which has always existed in Dudley Hill is still well and truly alive, and there are those who look back fondly on the 'old days' and who have set down their memories for the benefit of current and future generations, via the excellent publications of the Dudley Hill Local History Group.

**Further Reading**

**Bridgeland, Gina (Ed.)** *Dudley Hill: Memories of a Bygone Age* Dudley Hill Local History Group, 1991.

The Picture Palace, Dudley Hill, was known locally as 't 'Dud'. It opened in 1912 and entertained people for over 50 years. *(M. Birdsall)*

The crossroads at Dudley Hill, pictured in 1960. *(Mabel Bruce)*

The Sunday school and burial ground on Dudley Street in 1965. *(Mabel Bruce)*

This picture, from 1969, clearly illustrates the effects of the road schemes in the Dudley Hill area. The Picture Palace is on the left. *(Bradford Libraries)*

# East Bierley

William the Conqueror created Ilbert de Lacy Baron of Pontefract in 1070 and, with this, granted him the Manor of Bierley among others as a reward for services in the conquest. In all de Lacy possessed 150 manors in the West Riding of Yorkshire. At the time Bierley was worth 10 shillings, and comprised four carucates (about 400 acres) of land with two ploughs.

Bierley Manor consisted of North and East Bierley, but as early as 1316, East Bierley became a separate manor. James Parker believed that William Pollard, a member of one of the oldest Bierley families, who lived at the old Manor House, sold the Manor of Bierley to the Richardson family of North Bierley and Bierley Hall.

The name Bierley is defined as low land adjoining a 'byre'. In Cudworth's time, East Bierley was less populated than the North Bierley township. It consisted of the hill slopes rising from Low Moor towards Bradford, bounded by the old township limits of Bolling. From the names Upper and Lower Woodlands, we can infer that these hill slopes were once covered by forest, hence another name reference to *ley*, meaning settlement in a clearing of woodland. The farmhouses of Woodhouse Hill and Bierley combined agriculture with woollen, and later, worsted cloth domestic manufacture. By 1891, however, the population had increased, new industry had developed and nearly all the male inhabitants were employed in mining, 'clogging it to work', or were employed at the local ironworks. Women and children found work in the neighbouring worsted mills.

Bradford coal was mined as early as mediaeval times and consisted of a valuable range mined in shallow pits throughout the dale and local moorland. East Bierley was fortunate in having both types of coal, which provided the most economic mining of coal and minerals. In 1906, Bierley was part of the Low Moor system of collieries, mineral railways and waggonways. Most of the coal was consumed locally. The rich beds of Bierley included Black Bed ironstone. Joseph Fieldhouse speculated that iron could have been transported from Bierley mines and forges as early as Roman times along a road from Drighlington to Tong Street, shown by the Ordnance Survey map of Roman Britain. Dr Richard Richardson, of Bierley Hall, also found Roman coins in a heap of cinders on his estate in the 1700s, and other similar finds were made in neighbourhood slag heaps. Not surprisingly, Bierley had its own iron works in the 19th century, begun around 1810 by Nathaniel Aked of Bradford. Shortly after, the business was considerably extended by the Leah family who, in partnership with James Marshall, ironmonger of Kirkgate, had purchased the business. In 1854, it was bought by the Low Moor company who concentrated the works on the manufacture of pig iron, in keeping with that company's own production. According to

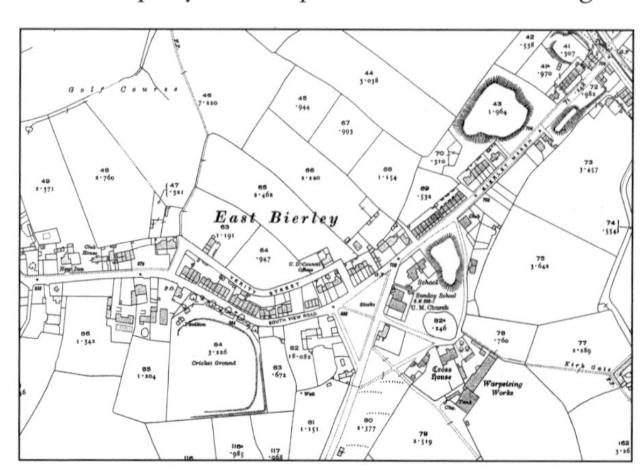

East Bierley, shown on a map from 1922.

East Bierley village green, with stocks. *(Pete Walker)*

C. Richardson, work at Bierley ended in the early 1880s and the works were pulled down in 1889. The 1852 6in to 1 mile Ordnance Survey map of Bradford shows its coal and ironstone pits like indentations on a lunar landscape.

One of the oldest properties remaining in the village is Cross House. It was built in 1662 and occupied by the Rhodes family for about 200 years. It is thought to have obtained its name from the nearby site of an ancient cross at which church services were once held. All that remains of the cross is what is known in the village as the Cup and Saucer, which are two large stones, one on top of the other. It is said that when the weather was bad, services were then held at Cross House. East Bierley's manor house, Moor House, is now a private home. The house was built in 1652 and was the home of the Willeys family, who were mainly woolstaplers and worsted spinners.

Mention must also be made of Bierley Hall, which sadly has not remained, but was for a long time quite a source of news both inside and outside the village. According to William Cudworth, Bierley Hall was built in 1636 by the Richardsons. It underwent considerable alteration during its time, and an Italianate façade was added. The staircase hall had a rococo ceiling with emblems including those of sculpture and architecture. The gardens included lakes, a grotto and even a druids' circle, fish ponds and the second hothouse to be built in England. A photograph of the hall and a sketch made in 1720 can be seen in *Lost Houses of the West Riding*. By 1800, the hall was tenanted – it had been bought by Bradford Corporation to be used as a hospital for infectious diseases. It was later an old peoples' hospital, before being demolished in the late 1960s. Among the most notable of the Richardson family residents was Richard Richardson MD FRS (1663–1781), botanist, natural scientist and church builder. In 1712, he was elected a Fellow of the Royal Society of Medicine and was well known in the scientific and intellectual circles of his day. Under his guidance and knowledge, the gardens flourished and were said to be among the finest in the north. He built the hothouse and also planted the famous Cedar of Lebanon, which used to stand in front of the hall. In 1816 its

The duck pond, East Bierley village. *(Pete Walker)*

circumference was over 12ft but it was cut down in 1907. The tree was sent to Richardson in about 1705 by Sir Hans Sloane, president of the Royal Society and a good friend. Dr Richardson also built Bierley Chapel in 1766 in the Grecian style of architecture. It became a parish church in 1864. Dr Richardson's extensive correspondence was published in the 19th century.

Another notable member of the Richardson family was Miss Frances Richardson Currer. She collected a very large and valuable library, later sold in London, and added to the family's collection of prints, shells and fossils. It was also Miss Currer who initially leased the land for the Bierley Ironworks. She died in 1861, having held the estates for 76 years.

The village of East Bierley is probably the one in Bradford which most characterises the traditional rural vision of what a village should constitute. Tucked away between Tong Street and Birkenshaw, it has no busy major road through the centre of it, has its own village green with stocks, a large duck pond, an old well, a school, pub, church and golf club. The cricket team which goes back several generations won the National Village Championship in 1979 and more than 2,000 people turned up to cheer them on. Remarkably, East Bierley is only a stone's throw away from the busy M62 motorway, but thanks to the activities of the residents and their East Bierley Village Preservation Society, it has successfully conserved the core of the village and its society.

**Further Reading**

**Cudworth, William** *Round About Bradford* Queensbury Mountain Press, Bradford, 1968.

**Fieldhouse, Joseph** *Bradford* Watmoughs Limited & City of Bradford MC, Libraries Division, 1981.

**Parker, James** *Illustrated Rambles from Hipperholme to Tong* Percy Lund, Humphries & Co. Ltd, The Country Press, Bradford, 1904.

**Richardson, C.** *A Geography of Bradford* University of Bradford, 1976.

**Waterson, Edward and Peter Meadows** *Lost Houses of the West Riding* Jill Raines, York, 1998.

The Greenwood Inn, Bierley Lane, *c.*1900. *(Bradford Libraries)*

Bierley Chapel, pictured in 1899. *(Bradford Libraries)*

Bierley Hall, demolished in 1968. *(Bradford Libraries)*

Crosses House, East Bierley, *c.*1900. *(Bradford Libraries)*

# ECCLESHILL

ECCLESHILL occupies an elevated position a couple of miles north of Bradford city centre. Within its boundaries are included areas such as Fagley and Greengates, which are substantial enough to have their own entries in this book, and the vast estates of Thorpe Edge and Ravenscliffe. This is quite a bold statement as the actual area that makes up Eccleshill is something of a matter of controversy. In *Memories of Eccleshill*, the Eccleshill Local History Group suggest that 'the boundaries form a rough triangle, with its base at the west (Bolton) and its apex at the north-east (Apperley Bridge).' They are a lot more specific in naming streets and becks that form the actual boundaries with neighbouring districts. Bradford council sets out a description of what constitutes the official area of Eccleshill ward in its ward profile for the district. 'Eccleshill is a predominantly residential ward stretching out from Five Lane Ends to open country to form the boundary with Leeds'.

If the boundaries of Eccleshill are something of a puzzle, then the various spellings and meanings of its name are another matter entirely. At different times in its recorded history the village has been called Egleshill, Ecckleshill and Heckeshill, to name but three. Vera Taylor covers the subject of Eccleshill's name and its meaning in *Eccleshill in Times Past*.

Eccleshill (as Egleshill) merits a mention in the Domesday Book, which states that it consisted of 300 acres of land, held in the manor of Wakefield. Eccleshill Manor passed through the hands of various owners, including the Sheffields (of Sheffield, not surprisingly), George Zouche (1552), Walter Calverley (until 1560), before eventually passing into the possession of the Hirds of Apperley Lane who sold it to one Jeremiah Rawson in 1825. Today Eccleshill is in the ownership of many hundreds of private individuals as well as Bradford Council, which owns large portions of the ward in the form of council estates.

The township of Eccleshill retained its independence from Bradford for longer than many other areas in the district. It was not until 9 November 1899 that it was finally incorporated into the city, no doubt after a fierce 'independence' campaign by its inhabitants. The resident population seem to have been a feisty lot during the 19th century, opposing much of what they saw as unnecessary change, including the adoption of the Public Health Act in 1855, which was designed to bring them improved sanitary conditions.

The manufacture of cloth, and later worsted, was the prevalent trade in the township, and Eccleshill, like many other areas in the locale, could boast more than one mill, including Old Mill and Moorside Mill. In the early part of the 19th century much work was carried out in the home, of course, and Eccleshill was no exception. Excellent examples of weavers' cottages are still in existence at Moorwell Place, by the recreation ground.

The 20th century saw a huge increase in housing developments in the area, and most of the farmland and open fields that once surrounded Eccleshill were soon swallowed up. To the west of the ward are the smart, leafy 1930s developments, which surround Norman Avenue, and to the south lies the similar Leafield estate. The east of the ward is taken up with the Ravenscliffe and Greengates estates, archetypal 1960s local authority housing estates of a similar design to Thorpe Edge, which lies along Eccleshill's northern edge. The new housing estates, and developments such as Morrisons' vast Enterprise Five complex at Five Lane Ends have helped to shift the centre of gravity of Eccleshill away from the original village centre, and have undoubtedly contributed to its progress, if that is the right word, into a fully fledged suburb of Bradford. Indeed statistics show that in 1991, although the ward only covered 1.1 miles, the population was 14,900. Nearly 30 percent of the households were living in council-owned accommodation, mainly on the aforementioned estates, and almost one quarter of the children in the ward lived in lone-parent families. Socially, as well as physically, Eccleshill has changed dramatically over the last 50 years or so, although the district could be considered fortunate in that the original 'core' of the village is still very much in evidence.

A walk through the village illustrates just how much of old Eccleshill has survived the 20th century's development. Standing at the bottom of Stone Hall Road, with Pullan Avenue and its smart 1930s dwellings to the left, one can look past the library to see the early 1990s housing development built on the site of an old quarry. Behind the library is where the old Manor Pottery once stood. Firebricks, chimney pots and sewerage pipes were among the wares produced at this pottery, which was opened in about 1837 by Jeremiah Rawson, then Lord of the Manor. Walking up Stone Hall Road one passes the Prospect pub on the right-hand side. Once a private residence, this large, friendly pub lies in its own grounds and has recently been extended. Next to the Prospect lies Eccleshill recreation ground, which was originally Eccleshill Common, and was granted to the township in 1848. In 1864 it was legally established that it must forever remain for the free use of the township's people, and it has been a popular gathering place for generations of children ever since. The 'rec', as it is commonly known, has a bowling green and club at one end, and along its bottom edge runs the aforementioned Moorwell Place, with its weavers' cottages, named after the Moor Well, which once stood nearby. The 'moor' theme is carried on by Moorside Road, which forms a boundary to the rec. At the northern end of the rec stands the Eccleshill war memorial, which honours the villagers lost in the two World Wars.

Further up Stone Hall Road, on the left, is Stonehall Mill, built for H.R. Halstead in the mid-19th century. Beyond the mill stands the original Prospect Hotel, built in 1869 and once a popular watering hole for generations of villagers. Now, still popular, it is home to a betting shop. At the very top of Stone Hall Road, at its junction with Moorside Road, is a cluster of ancient cottages, a reminder of how many of the village's dwellings must have once looked. Opposite stands the Mechanics' Institute, built in 1869 for the Mutual Improvement Society. Over the years this imposing building has had many uses, including cinema, dance hall and village library. When the new Eccleshill library, at the top of Pullan Avenue, was opened in 1964, the Mechanics' Institute was used by Bradford Museums as a storage facility. Nowadays it is a thriving community centre, used by many local groups including the popular Eccleshill Local History Society.

At the top of the village Stone Hall Road joins with Stoney Lane, which runs down through the heart of old Eccleshill, and reputedly earned its name in ancient times when the locals stoned to death a missionary, or monk. Many of the old shops and cottages which line Stoney Lane have survived the years intact, and lend Eccleshill something of an 'olde world' charm. At the bottom of Stoney Lane, at

Shops and cottages on Stoney Lane, at the heart of Eccleshill village. *(M. Birdsall)*

the junction with Victoria Road, is a raised pavement known locally as the Monkey Bridge, under which the village lock-up was once located. Norman Lane runs to Five Lane Ends from here, and near to its junction with Stoney Lane stood Prospect Chapel, built in 1775. John Wesley once preached at the chapel, which in recent years ended up being used as a joiner's workshop and undertaker's premises.

Running in the opposite direction from Norman Lane is Victoria Road, at the far end of which stands St Luke's, Eccleshill's parish church, with its strange-looking tower. Opposite the church is the Ring O' Bells pub, formerly named the Hammer and Anvil after the blacksmith's which stood on the site of the church. Whoever decided to rename the pub obviously hadn't done their homework – St Luke's has never had any bells to ring.

Eccleshill's most famous son is surely David Hockney, the world-renowned artist. The Hockney family moved to a terraced house in Hutton Terrace in 1943. David attended the Wellington Road Primary and Junior School and on a Sunday was a regular at the Victoria Road Methodist Church, where he apparently shocked the Sunday School teachers by drawing cartoons of Jesus. Imagine how much those drawings would be worth today!

All in all, the township of Eccleshill, despite the massive housing developments that have eaten up much of its open space, has managed

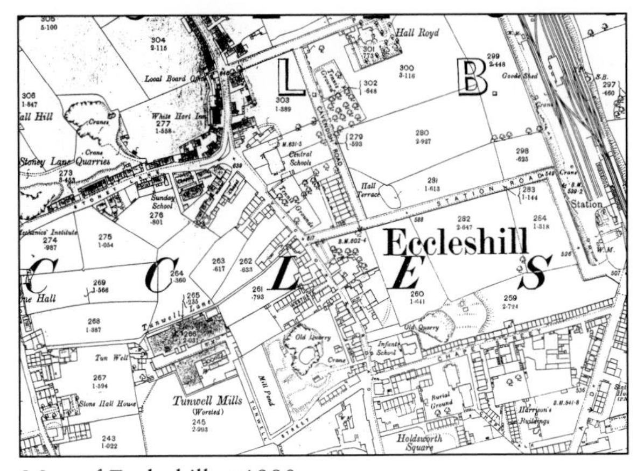


Map of Eccleshill, *c.*1890.

to retain at its core many of its original features and charm. Walking up Stoney Lane one can easily picture how the village must have looked in earlier times. Eccleshill has certainly outgrown its rural, village roots, but if you know where to look, glimpses of that old Eccleshill can still be found.

Eccleshills Mechanics' Institute, built in 1868, stands at the top of the village. *(Gina Szekely)*

**Further Reading**
**Cudworth, William** *Round About Bradford,* 1876. (Reproduced 1968, Arthur Dobson Publishing Co.)
**Eccleshill Local History Group** *History Trail of Eccleshill In 1899* Eccleshill LHG, 1999.
**Eccleshill Local History Group** *Memories of Eccleshill* Leeds University, 1990.

Known locally as the 'Monkey Bridge', the remains of Eccleshill's lock-up can be clearly seen. *(M. Birdsall)*

Ancient cottages at the junction of Moorside Road and Stoney Lane. *(Ann Birdsall)*

Farmland once lay on the present site of the Ravenscliffe Estate (date unkown). *(Bradford Libraries)*

Wesleyan Sunday school, Eccleshill. Artist David Hockney attended as a child. *(Ann Birdsall)*

Mechanics' Institute, Eccleshill. It is now used as a community centre. *(Ann Birdsall)*

Averingcliffe Farm, Eccleshill, was built in 1610. It was demolished in 1951 to make way for the Thorpe Edge Estate (date unknown). *(Bradford Libraries)*

Eccleshill Bank before demolition and road widening. A hoard of gold was found in the farmhouse on the left during demolition (date unknown). *(Bradford Libraries)*

The original Ring of Bells pub, Harrogate Road. The pub took its name from St Luke's Church across the road, even though it has never had any bells! (date unknown). *(Bradford Libraries)*

Lock-up Hill, Eccleshill. Primitive Methodism in Eccleshill began in one of the cottages (date unknown). *(Bradford Libraries)*

# FAGLEY

FAGLEY is a suburb of Bradford with a population of 4,734. It is situated to the north-east of the city centre, with Fagley Beck forming the boundary with Calverley. Fagley was originally part of the township of Eccleshill and became part of the city of Bradford in 1899. There are various theories as to where the name Fagley originates from. The most common explanation comes from the Old English *fag*, which simply means multi-coloured. And the common suffix -ley comes from the Old English *leah*, meaning a clearing in the woodland. It seems strange to perceive Fagley as a 'multi-coloured clearing in the woodland' nowadays.

Fagley, like many other suburbs of Bradford, has two very different faces. It enjoys all the amenities of big city life while having abundant greenery nearby. It is a bit of a 'mish-mash' of a place really. There are quaint old cottages, Victorian terraced houses, a post-war council estate, old farmsteads on winding country lanes, picturesque streams and acres of green fields and woodland.

The main thoroughfare through the area is Fagley Road, which runs down from Killinghall Road to Fagley Beck. This used to be a small country lane, frequented by horse and cart. Nowadays, its busy junction with Killinghall Road is home to many shops and businesses. The road runs from this busy junction, down through the Fagley estate towards the Blue Pig public house. This hostelry has been there for over a century. It was originally called the Ravenscliffe Hotel. Alcohol has been sold on the site for even longer though. There used to be a whistling shop here, where folk could buy their spirits out of hours. They were sold through a small window poised perilously close to Fagley Brook. Local bobbies had a hard time of it when trying to bring the law breakers to justice. They could never tell whether you were in Fagley or Calverley when the money changed hands. The Ravenscliffe was built on this site. No one is quite sure why the pub changed its name to the Blue Pig. There are theories that it got its new name because the landlord used to keep cross-bred pigs which had a bluey/grey skin. Others believe that a local farmer played a joke on the regulars there. He arrived at the hotel with a pig which had just been born on the farm, but had painted it a bright shade of blue to fool his friends. The pub was known as the Blue Pig ever since.

One of the area's landmarks is St Clare's Roman Catholic Church, on Moorside Road. This busy church is built on the site of an old tower, which itself was a notable landmark, though not for religious reasons. The tower was built by Benjamin Farrer, a wool dealer, in 1828. It was built as a memorial to the Jobson family, who had left Farrer a small fortune. It became known as the 'spy' tower and was a popular meeting place for courting couples and playful kids. Some lads used to dress up as ghosts with sheets over their heads to scare off the courting couples. Sadly, the tower became so dilapidated that it was eventually demolished in 1925, although some still believe a storm caused it to collapse at around the same time. The tower was once occupied by a fishmonger, who had one of the floors in the late 19th century.

Another of Fagley's historic landmarks has also been affected by the passage of time. The ford across Fagley Beck, which used to be on the route of the ancient Bradford to Leeds toll road, had to be replaced by a more modern

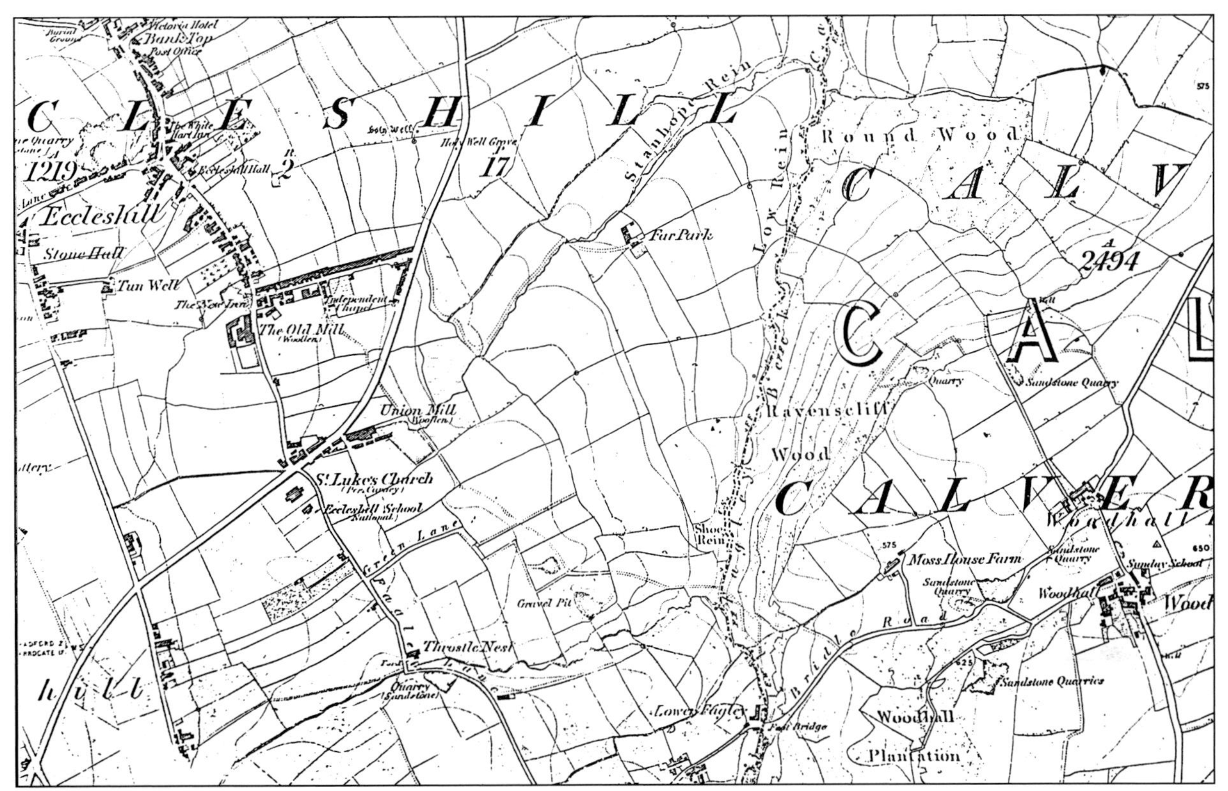


Map showing the small settlements of Upper and Lower Fagley in 1852.

The Blue Pig public house, Fagley, 2002. *(Gina Szekely)*

crossing because of its dangerous state. The old flags of Yorkshire stone were replaced with newer ones, and many locals were not happy with this. They believed the council were tinkering with history, and changing the ford's 'old world' appearance. They fought the plan but were defeated in 1990. It seems Fagley folk do not take things lying down. Their fighting spirit is personified by one Eric Anderson, the only Bradford-born man to be awarded the Victoria Cross in World War Two. The cross was awarded posthumously for supreme valour. A stone tablet in memory of Eric Anderson was placed on the walls of Fagley Congregational Church. He was killed while serving with the Duke of York's Own Regiment in North Africa.

Fagley today still shows some of the signs of the past, and there is still evidence of why people settled in this sheltered valley in the first place. The fertile farming land still exists, as do the remains of the quarries that populated the area. Many of these disused quarries have now been taken over by flora and fauna. The building of the Fagley estate and the encroachment of the Ravenscliffe estate have changed the character of the area for good, but Fagley still backs on to green fields and its proximity to the city centre means it will always remain a popular suburb with one foot in the city and one foot in the countryside.

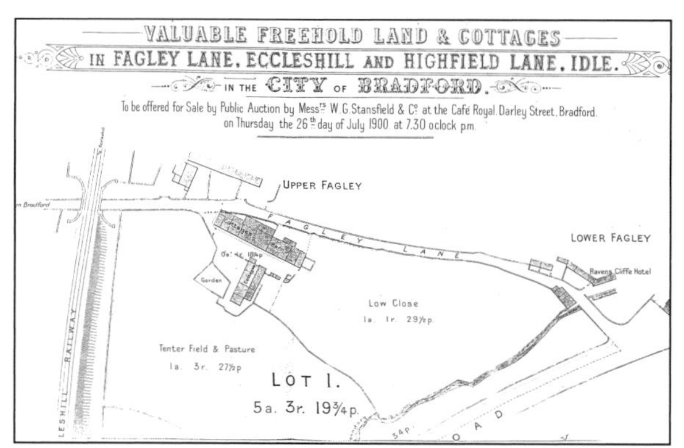

Sale plan for land on Fagley Lane, 1900, with the Ravenscliffe Hotel, now the Blue Pig, at the bottom of the lane. *(Bradford Libraries)*

**Further Reading**

**Eccleshill Local History Group** *A Ramble Round Fagley* Eccleshill Local History Group, 1995.

# FRIZINGHALL

FRIZINGHALL lies between Manningham and Shipley and is intersected by the busy old Bradford Road to Saltaire, Bingley, Keighley and Skipton. Because of its position between Shipley and Bradford it was once controlled by two separate authorities.

Frizinghall has had a few names over the years, such as Fresinghal, Fresinghale and Frysynghall. According to William Cudworth, the name derives from the coarse woollen cloth called 'frieze' which was made in the hamlet. *Frieze* is a Celtic word for a nap of cloth. The settlement is mentioned as early as 1287, when it is described as belonging to Robert de Everingham, Lord of the Manor of Heaton. It was originally one of the largest outlying hamlets of Heaton.

There were two working mills in Frizinghall. Frizinghall Mill was originally used for corn and as a fulling mill. In 1818, after a fire, it was rebuilt and was taken for worsted spinning by William and Joseph Hargreaves, who employed a large number of hand-weavers. Their father James Hargreaves moved from Delph Hill to live at the Old Castle, Frizinghall, in 1779, a large old house belonging to the Listers. Dumb Mill was originally a corn mill under Benjamin Spence, miller, in 1762, but was bought by Joseph Wood, a small clothmaker of Shipley Fields who built the worsted mill. His three sons expanded the business as Benjamin Wood & Co.

Among locally famous names, Mary Hargreaves, sister of Mr Joseph Hargreaves of Frizinghall Mill, was a clever business woman who was the partner of Joseph Wood, clothmaker, and later ran her own worsted trade at Mill House. Another notable was William or Willie Wilson (1767–1849), descendant of an American Quaker family and a renowned philanthropist. As well as his charity work against poverty, he was president of the Bradford Temperance Society, which was the first to be established in England.

Frizingley Old Hall was built by James Lister in 1727 on the site of a much older building. The village was grouped around this. According to William Cudworth, the hall stood on 'a little knoll, surrounded by some grand old trees' in his time. It was then occupied by Mr Benjamin Wood, the manufacturing 'squire' of the village, on lease from the Marriner family of Keighley, into which the Listers later married. In the 19th century it was extended into Frizingley Hall, later a private residence just off Frizinghall Road. Jacob Behrens once lived there. He founded Bradford High School, which was amalgamated with Bradford Grammar School in 1873. He is also reported to have installed the first domestic bath in the area. Bradford Grammar School stands at the top of Frizinghall Road, opposite Lister Park. It is one of Yorkshire's most famous independent schools. Its Royal Charter was granted in 1662 but records suggest the school existed before then. In 1655 the school's lands in Manningham were estimated at more than 15 acres. In January 1949, the Duke of Edinburgh opened the new school opposite Lister Park, an event which had been delayed due to the war. Among its famous ex-pupils are Frederick Delius, David Hockney and Jonathan Silver.

Today Frizinghall is neither the village nor the shopping centre it once was. In November 1963 it was described by a *Telegraph & Argus* journalist as having all the shops necessary for the family's day-to-day shopping. It still has a post office, chemist and the odd corner shop but nothing like the number and quality it used to have. However, its position on one of the busiest roads means that specialist businesses, such as the model railway shop, can continue, and as a location it still attracts take-away businesses and restaurants. Pubs in Frizinghall are as popular as ever with the Old Barn, which dates back to 1610 and the Park, formerly known as the Turf Tavern, which is mentioned in Cudworth. The Black Swan (known locally as the 'Mucky Duck') is very old and was once kept by a Mally Rhodes who had a lucrative sideline as a midwife.

Nevertheless, apart from nearby Lister Park, today Frizinghall itself has nothing compared to the Alfresco Pavilion once situated on the derelict land at the top of Frizinghall Road by the grammar school. This was a centre for concert party and music hall entertainment between 1908 and 1920, with shows once advertised as twice daily at 3pm and 7.30pm. Here Matt Kilduff held his Sequins concert parties, which were popular enough to tour in 1918, using the Alfresco as a base. The Pavilion later became a filling station, then a Vauxhall and later a Renault dealership. It was not until 1991 that it was demolished.

Frizinghall is still a leafy area, handsome in parts, especially around Park Grove and Heaton Grove, up to Heaton Woods. Here, the middle and professional classes moved from the city in the late 19th century, as public transport to Bradford improved. Frizinghall still has many beautiful large houses, some using half-timbering with long snow roofs, as on the Heaton Grove estate (*c.*1872 ) and noted by George Sheeran in *The Victorian Houses of Bradford*. Other villas in Park Grove are some of the finest examples of Arts and Crafts design in Bradford, built between 1891–5 by H. & E. Marten, local architects.

Today Frizinghall has a multi-ethnic mix with a fairly large South Asian population and a smaller Eastern European population, residents for many years. Bradford's first purpose-built multicultural community centre was opened in Midland Road in 1985 to serve Asians, Italians, Irish and Poles among others. Projects have included a 'green' library, to encourage people to borrow books and learn about DIY and gardening, a youth club and mothers' and children's groups. Although it has never attracted the broad ethnic mix it hoped for, it still provides a valuable service. There is still a pride in the area and a desire to maintain a community feel. The Frizinghall Community Centre has established a range of projects to spruce up the area, provides children's activities, IT training, homework clubs and sessions on drugs awareness.

Frizinghall's good transport communications should also ensure that the area never suffers from the prospect of a terminal decline, as in many former villages facing the competition of nearby supermarkets. Even the railway station, closed since 1965, continues to serve its populace, having been reopened in 1987 to the sound of a jazz band and the vision of a huge iced cake.

**Further Reading**

**Appleby, Jim and Jim Greenhalf** *Telegraph & Argus Stories of the Century* The Breedon Books Publishing Company Limited, Derby, 1999.

**Cudworth, William** *Round About Bradford, Queensbury* Mountain Press, Bradford, 1968.

**Robinson, Lilian** *Facts about Frizinghall,* 1975

**Sheeran, George** *The Victorian Houses of Bradford* Bradford Libraries and Information Service, Bradford, 1990.

The New Church, off Keighley Road, Frizinghall. *(Gina Szekely)*

Restaurants: Orlando's and the Bengal Brasserie, and the long standing Frizinghall Models and Railways shop, at the top of Frizinghall Road. *(M. Birdsall)*

The popular Black Swan, known locally as the 'Mucky Duck', was once kept by midwife Mally Rhodes. *(Gina Szekely)*

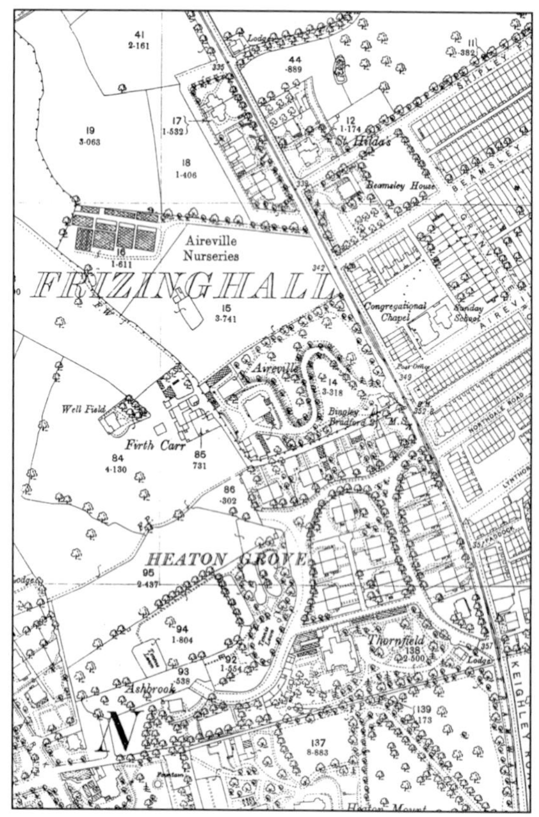


Frizinghall shown on a map from the 1890s.

The laying of the foundation stone for the Institution for the Blind, 22 September 1920. Mr Frederick Priestnal presides. *(Bradford Libraries)*

Heaton Grove, Frizinghall, noted for its unusual houses and also the pre-1862 site of a scheme for out-of-work wool sorters, which included allotments, baths and teahouses. *(Gina Szekely)*

This picture was taken in 1860, and shows the Wesleyan Sunday School and Chapel in Frizinghall. *(Bradford Libraries)*

# GIRLINGTON

GIRLINGTON is situated to the west of Bradford city centre and can be described as lying in the rough triangle formed by Toller and Duckworth Lanes to the north and Thornton Road to the south. Its heart is probably close to the junction of Thornton and Ingleby Roads and Whetley Lane, but with no official boundaries to work to the reader may well find their own, differing theories as to where Girlington begins and ends. The area derives its name from the Gaelic word for rough ground, *gir*, in which heather, *ling*, grows. *Ton* was the term for a settlement.

Although the term Girlington has been in existence for many years (Cudworth mentions it appearing in old records) it would seem that the bustling, built up community so well-known to modern Bradfordians is not as old as many of the other suburbs in the city. In his *Histories of Manningham, Heaton and Allerton* (published 1896) the aforementioned Mr Cudworth describes the 'thriving colony' at Girlington as being non-existent in the early years of the 19th century. A homestead bearing the name Girlington once stood where Kensington Street now lies, but otherwise the area was virtually empty, save for an occupation road which briefly crossed part of it.

The Girlington estate, such as it was, was acquired in 1850–2 by the Bradford Freehold Land Society, which had formed in 1849 with Sir Titus Salt as its president. The idea behind this philanthropic movement was that the society would acquire land and then sell it at reasonable prices to people who would otherwise never be able to afford their own homes. Even the humblest of men should be able to meet the monthly repayments, and the ultimate aim of the society was that these men would then build their own homes on the plot they had bought. Around 250 plots were made available in Girlington, in an area covering roughly 30 acres, and they varied in price, with the best-positioned plots costing up to 5s per square yard.

Thus Girlington was opened up for building, although at first it took on something of a 'straggled' appearance, with single-storey dwellings dotted around. To the people living in Girlington at this time, the place seemed a long way from the town of Bradford, and the only means of actually getting there was on foot, or, if one was lucky, by hitching a lift on a passing milk-cart. Back then the Girlington area was noted for its coal mines, and one business near to Four Lane Ends, opened by Messrs Hardcastle, Aked and Co., employed about 150 men. 'Bell mines', or small, open mines in which several men could dig for coal, were used across this particular area, and one was found in the 1980s during the construction of a temporary classroom at St Phillip's School in Girlington Road. Research by teachers and pupils dated that particular mine back as far as the 1840s. The mines eventually closed down and the progress of building development in Girlington quickened until by the end of the 19th century the area had emerged as a thriving suburb of the city.

The four main streets in Girlington at the time were Kensington, Girlington and Washington Streets and St Leonard's Road, and the housing ranged from small back-to-backs to large detached properties. Many shops and businesses established in Girlington at this time lasted well into the 20th century, such as J. Robinson, herbalist, who traded in the area for many years.

Little Lane Congregational Sunday school, Girlington. This illustration appeared in the *Illustrated Weekly Telegraph*, 16 February 1889. *(Bradford Libraries)*

The early years of the 20th century saw much unemployment and hardship and Bradford, with its many industries, was not spared. By 1905, with the government of the day seemingly incapable of doing anything to ease the situation, feelings were running high and people began to take matters into their own hands. What happened in Girlington was probably the most remarkable chapter in that area's history. Orators had already begun to advocate a 'return to the land', where men could produce their own food supplies and make a living by their own efforts. In the desperate, beleaguered men of Bradford they found a willing audience. A Mr Glyde led a meeting at Morley Street and a decision was made to 'grab' a piece of land on which to live and work, in a similar fashion to events that were already under way in Manchester. The piece of land chosen was in Girlington, (in Whetley Lane), belonged to the Midland Railway Company and was currently lying idle. The land was 'grabbed' in late July and tents were quickly erected for the fifteen men involved to live in. The soil was tilled and crops planted, the men carrying out their labours on a meagre diet of little more than bread and weak tea.

'Klondike Villas', as the camp became known, quickly caught the attention of the general public, and the men became minor celebrities. The Midland Railway Company was less than impressed, however, and soon began legal proceedings to reclaim its land. The land grabbers erected a more permanent structure of timber and turf and announced they would sell their crops for a profit, once they were

Whetley Lane unemployment camp, home to the land grabbers. The man on the left is identified as Mr Stewart Gray, 1906. *(Bradford Libraries)*

harvested. As the weeks passed, however, public opinion began to change. The camp's sanitation, it was claimed, was injurious to the health of the neighbourhood, and morale at the camp, already low, was shattered by the failure of the crops. By late October, faced with a long winter in a cold, leaky hut, the men finally admitted bitter defeat and disbanded their camp. The case of the Girlington land grabbers was over; their high hopes and hard work were ultimately for nothing. The Midland Railway Company reclaimed its land and stopped legal proceedings.

The second half of the 20th century saw many changes in and around the Girlington area. The make up of its population changed substantially, with many families from ethnic minorities choosing to make their homes in the district, firstly Eastern Europeans, in the early 1960s, followed by people from the Indian sub-continent. All were attracted to the district by the prospect of a better life, whether it be to escape persecution in their homelands or to seek employment in Bradford's mills. Indeed it would be probably be fair to say that well over half of Girlington's resident population is now of Asian origin.

Shops have come and gone. Morrisons opened a large store near Four Lane Ends, creating a shopping complex which now includes other retail outlets. The historic Victoria Buildings, a much-loved terrace of shops, was lost to the bulldozers in the mid-1990s despite fierce local opposition. The Bradford Royal Infirmary up on Duckworth Lane has led to Girlington's inhabitants having to become familiar with the scream of ambulances tearing through their midst.

The 'Back to the Land' land grabbers set up camp in Girlington in 1906. Their efforts to make a living for themselves by selling crops and produce from their camp were ultimately unsuccessful. *(Bradford Libraries)*

The people of Girlington can be justly proud of their district, with its excellent facilities – shopping centres, places of worship for all faiths, pubs, clubs and community centres, and there are groups such as the Girlington Action Partnership and the Bradford West Area Panel which seek to work with the community to improve facilities and standards of life. An example of the community working with such bodies to improve the area came in December 1999 with the unveiling of a mosaic for all in Girlington to enjoy. The mosaic was initiated by the aforementioned Action Partnership, designed by local children and funded in part by local businesses. The then Lord Mayor, Councillor Peter Lancaster, opened the mosaic at a ceremony attended by pupils of Girlington and St Phillip's Primary Schools. This is definitely a splendid example of a community working together for the good of all, and indicative of the spirit of Girlington.

**Further Reading**

**Cudworth, William** *Histories of Manningham, Heaton and Allerton,* 1896.
**McDermott, Michael** *West of Bradford* Michael McDermott, 1991.

# GREENGATES

SITUATED around three miles north of Bradford, Greengates is unfairly known by many as no more than the busy Bradford to Harrogate and Leeds to Keighley crossroads. Its boundaries, however, spread beyond this busy junction. The actual parish boundaries show that Greengates includes parts of the Thorpe Edge and Ravenscliffe estates and Apperley Bridge. The population of Greengates (including Ravenscliffe) is 5,218.

Greengates is not an ancient village with its roots going back to Saxon times. It is simply a village of the Victorian era, built with the grey Yorkshire stone of early Victorian prosperity. In fact little of Greengates nowadays is more than 50 years old.

The village, like many others in Bradford, has now been swallowed up by the city. However, some of the prettier and more interesting qualities of the place still exist. Take, for example, the row of cottages in Stockhill Fold. They were built for weavers and some date from as early as 1786. They were renovated in 1979. The builders and architects ensured that many of the original features were retained. In fact, Methodist pioneer John Wesley is reputed to have stayed in one of the cottages. They are all now listed buildings. Another of the village's most famous landmarks is its war memorial, situated at the busy crossroads. The imposing angel statue was erected in memory of the men of Greengates who died in World War One.

Some older people may still remember with affection Greengates's mills, or the acres and acres of green fields that surrounded the village before the arrival of the large housing estates in the area. Some people may also remember some of the district's characters. There was the hermit who lived on the moors of Thorpe Edge, before the estate was built there. He was known as 'Pit Dick', living in one of the old mines that used to be dotted all over the moor. His real name was Richard Bolton. Local lads used to tease him and pinch his possessions. The girls, though, were scared stiff of him.

Then there was Greengates's own 'Wee Willie Winkie', Joshie Cockey. He was employed as a 'knocker up' by the local mills. Some may remember the time when he knocked everyone up an hour early. When he realised his mistake he had to go back on his rounds letting folk know that they could have another hour in bed.

Greengates was a real centre for Methodism in Bradford. The first group met there in 1781, the year Wesley was supposed to have stayed in Stockhill Fold. Methodism prospered and meetings were held in a building in Haigh Hall Road. This building eventually became Greengates Library, as well as a burling and mending workshop.

Today Greengates can certainly be a bottleneck. The busy junction at its centre, known as New Line, is now under more pressure with the arrival of supermarkets and a small retail park. Next time you're doing your weekly shop in Sainsbury's, or travelling between Shipley and Leeds or Bradford and Harrogate, spare a thought for what used to be a small, quiet village, with superb views over the Aire Valley.

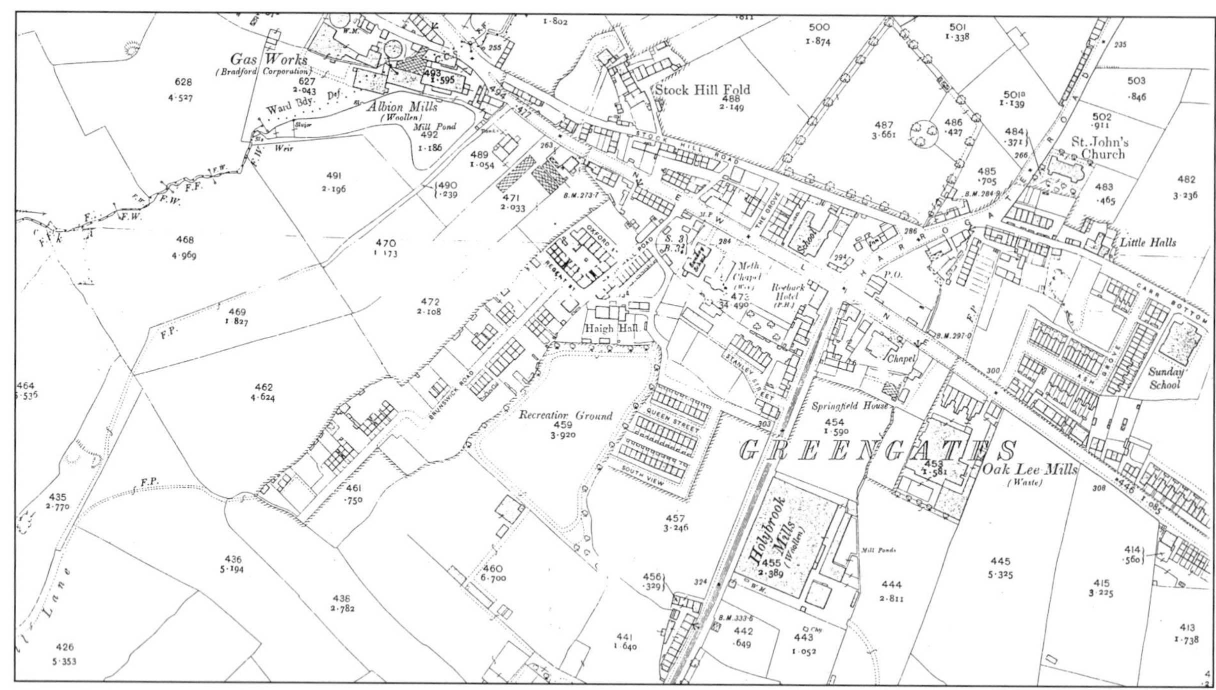


Map of Greengates, 1908.

Greengates war memorial, 2002, dedicated to those from the village who died in World War One. *(Pete Walker)*

Weaver's cottages in Stockhill Fold, 2002. It is rumoured that John Wesley stayed in one of the cottages. *(Pete Walker)*

Rows of cottages in Stockhill Road, 2002. *(Pete Walker)*

New Line, Greengates, in more peaceful times. *(Bradford Libraries)*

# Heaton

IN ATTEMPTING to write a short history and description of Heaton, one must first set down exactly what constitutes the physical area that Heaton covers. John Stanley King, one of Heaton's best-known 20th century sons, identified three differing interpretations of Heaton in his book *Heaton, the best place of all* (Bradford Libraries, 2001). Firstly there's the historic township of Heaton, independent from Bradford until 1882, then there's the modern-day council ward of Heaton, with its differing borders, a creation of the city of Bradford Metropolitan Council, and finally there's the somewhat vague Heaton of newspaper articles and estate agents' adverts.

William Cudworth had definite ideas of the extent of the township, claiming that it stretched from Dumb Mill at Frizinghall to Sandy Lane Bottom at Allerton. Who would argue? The word 'Heaton' also bears more than one explanation. Mr King suggests it is derived from the Anglo-Saxon *haeh-tun* meaning high farmstead, Cudworth gives it as 'the enclosure on the open moorland', again Anglo-Saxon, this time derived from *haeth* – where the heath grows.

The early history of Heaton is quite well documented, and remains of cremation urns dating back to the mid-Bronze Age (*c.*1500 BC) were found at Chellow Heights in 1921. Evidence also suggests that a Roman road may well have passed through Heaton on its way from Pontefract to Ribchester in Lancashire. Many of the later records that refer to Heaton concern themselves with the township's boundaries. As early as the 1370s, John of Gaunt, the Duke of Lancaster, had defined Heaton's boundary with Manningham, and it is surprising to learn that the Anglican parishes in the area use those same boundaries today, over 600 years later.

Throughout Heaton's history runs a list of names, some familiar well into the 20th century. The Wilmer Fields, by marriage part of the family of the Earls of Rosse; the Cappes, landowners in Heaton for at least 250 years up until the 18th century; and the Midgleys and Jowetts, the latter family retaining possession of land in Heaton into the 1940s. With the exception of the Fields, all these families were named on a lay subsidy of 1545, which set out the taxes they were due to pay. Heaton Hall, long-time seat of the Field family, was built at the start of the 18th century and was a fitting residence for the Lords of the Manor.

The trades carried out in Heaton over the years are diverse, yet typical of many of Bradford's suburbs: quarrying, farming, brewing and, of course, cloth. The village long maintained its ancient, rural feel, and its hilly location, overlooking Bradford dale, coupled with its reputation for clean air and clear water, gave its inhabitants the best gift of all – good health. The benefits of such a living environment are obvious and can be clearly illustrated by the gathering at Heaton Hall of 46 people aged between 70 and 94. This feat doesn't seem so noteworthy until one learns that the get-together took place in 1868, when the age of 94 was almost impossible to reach. The fact that so many people from one township had reached such ages must have seemed quite wondrous to the residents of a dirty, unhealthy town like Bradford. Perhaps it was this healthy reputation that led to so many of the wealthy, powerful wool barons of Bradford setting up their residences there, in large, proud houses. Indeed from 1870

St Bede's Grammar School, Heaton. *(M. Birdsall)*

onwards, Heaton was *the* place to live within the Bradford district. It had a distinctly rural feel, was only 10 minutes from the centre of Bradford and, perhaps most importantly, the prevailing wind blew the other way, carrying the smoke, smog and smells of Bradford's wool trade far from the noses of the town's new rich.

Heaton managed to retain its independence as a township, separate from and ungoverned by Bradford, until 1882. Prior to its being amalgamated with Bradford, the township had been governed by the Heaton Local Board, which had provided the township with a reservoir and pumping station, reinforcing the 'clean air, clean water' ethos. All things come to an end though, and Heatonites (or Old Heatonians, perhaps) must have felt a sense of inevitability about the amalgamation, and probably a feeling that things would never quite be the same again.

Things certainly began to change for Heaton in the 20th century as increasing development across the Bradford district took its inevitable toll. The land and property owned by the Rosse family was sold off in a series of sales in 1911. William Edward, 5th Earl of Rosse, had

St Barnabas's Church, Heaton. The vicarage can be seen behind the church (date unknown). *(Bradford Libraries)*

succeeded to the title in 1908, and it was he who initiated the sales. As a parting gesture he presented Heaton Hill recreation ground to Bradford Corporation, and sold Heaton Woods to them in a cut-price deal. He also stressed his hopes that his erstwhile tenants would be able to purchase the homes and land that they had formerly rented from him.

One of the first, most dramatic, and sad results of the sales was to affect Heaton Hall itself. The hall failed to attract its £10,000 asking price, so in the end 69 acres of High Park, plus the manorial rights, were sold off to Jonas Whitley, ex-mayor of Bradford. The tenants of the hall, a Mr and Mrs Illingworth, moved out in June 1912, upon the expiry of their lease, and the hall was left to stand dark, cold and empty, a pale shadow of its former self. The fine old building was finally demolished in 1939. Much of the sold-off land from the estate was to end up being used for housing projects, as slowly but surely Heaton's once plentiful open spaces were swallowed up.

Nowadays, Heaton boasts a population of about 17,000 (within the Bradford Council ward boundaries) of which over a quarter are of Asian descent. The district is still populated by many people who have lived there all their lives, and whose families have lived in Heaton for generations, but the wool magnates are long gone (as is much of their industry), their place taken by a vibrant mixture of students and families buying their first homes. The township has managed to retain something of a sense of timelessness, despite the changes in the make-up of its resident population. Highgate remains as the historic centre of Heaton, and well-kept houses with lovingly tended gardens abound on the lanes that run off this now busy thoroughfare.

St Bede's Grammar School is probably the best-known of the many excellent schools in Heaton, and occupies a central position in the village, close to where Heaton Hall once stood. Heaton justifiably retains its long-standing reputation as one of Bradford's more desirable suburbs, and its diverse population is well served with shops, schools, pubs and sporting facilities, including its well-known tennis club, formed in the 1920s. Heaton Woods could perhaps be described as one of the best assets that the township possesses, and people from across the Bradford district have enjoyed the superb walks along the restored paths that wind their way alongside the streams that run through the woods. The Heaton Woods Trust actively campaigns to attract volunteers to help maintain and protect the woods, which provide a much-needed relief in the built up outskirts of the city.

A sense of community spirit prevails in Heaton, and some of the villagers still look back, fondly, to Heaton's more independent past. In 1982, descendents of former Heaton Local Board members met in the Kings Arms pub to toast the 100th anniversary of the townships amalgamation with Bradford. Present at the festivities was Councillor John Stanley King, the aforementioned stalwart of Heaton's recent history, who has represented this ward on Bradford council since 1970. He was Bradford's Lord Mayor in 2000–01 and, fittingly, holds the title of Lord of the Manor of Heaton. One suspects that the Field family would be content to know that their manor is now in such safe, caring hands.

**Further Reading**

**Cudworth, William** *Histories of Manningham, Heaton and Allerton,* 1896

**Cudworth, William** *Round About Bradford,* 1876. (Reproduced 1968, Arthur Dobson Publishing Co.)

**King, John Stanley** *Heaton, the best place of all* Bradford Libraries, 2001.

Heaton Hall in the 1890s. This property was the long time seat of the Field Family. It was demolished in 1939. *(Bradford Libraries)*

Garth House, Heaton. This was known as the Manor House in Heaton, and bore the inscription 'I.G. 1681'. *(Bradford Libraries)*

# Horton

THE township of Horton, in a similar fashion to its near neighbour, Bowling, is made up of two distinct areas. The Little and Great Hortons sit side by side to the south and south-west of the city centre, sharing their name, but in many respects very different suburbs of Bradford. We shall first look briefly at the ancient history of the Horton township as a whole before examining the two different communities.

The Domesday Book refers to Horton as being dependent on the Manor of Bradford. The first person named in connection with Horton would seem to be Robert de Stapleton, who lived sometime during the reign of Henry II (1154–89) and whose son Hugh assumed the name 'Horton' after being granted substantial land by Robert de Lacy, then Lord of the Manor of Bradford. The Hortons held the Manor of Horton until the reign of Edward I (1272-1307), before it passed through the hands of two families whose names are familiar to Bradford's history. These families, the Leventhorps and the Lacies, held Horton until it was bought back by one Joshua Horton in 1640. One of the more interesting lords of the manor of Horton must be one Charles Horton Rhyss. He has been described as having led a somewhat erratic life, combining a career as a captain in the army with that of a comedian, using the stage name of Morton Price. He mostly worked in the US and Canada but performed in Bradford's theatres on several occasions. He eventually sold the manor to William Cousen in 1858.

Evidence exists to show that coal was both found and used in Horton as long ago as the mid-14th century, and similarly it can be assumed that the township possessed its own corn mill as early as 1311, when the lord of the manor 'amerced' some of his tenants for using the mill at nearby Bradford instead. Like other areas across the district, Horton's inhabitants made their living from a combination of farming and the manufacture of cloth and other fabrics.

It is strange to think nowadays that the Horton of the early 1800s was physically quite separate from Bradford. A long stretch of open fields separated the two, a dark, lonely highway the only means of passage. Highway robberies were not uncommon.

The Trafalgar Coach passed through Horton on its way to Manchester or Liverpool, and some of the local manufacturers ran their own 'Calico Coach' to convey their goods to Manchester. Cotton and later worsted were manufactured in Horton's many mills.

The township governed its own affairs over the years, although Cudworth complains that the lack of books or records relating to Horton's official business leaves a 'blank so far as parochial matters are concerned' prior to the 19th century. Horton, like Bowling and Manningham, joined with Bradford at its incorporation in 1847.

# Little Horton

LIKE other suburbs within the Bradford district, Little Horton has more than one physical incarnation. There is the village of Little Horton with its historic centre at Little Horton Green, behind the imposing All Saints Church, and then there is the Little Horton ward, a more modern creation of Bradford Council. The council ward is described as being compact and urban, covering only 1.1 square miles, straddling the southern part of inner city Bradford. It contains the village that gives it its name, parts of East and West Bowling, and a fringe area of the city centre. It is a culturally diverse ward, and at the 1991 census its population of 16,800 included 23.3 percent of Pakistani or Bangladeshi origin, 5.3 percent of Afro-Caribbean origin and 4.2 percent of Indian origin. Over 33 percent of the households at this time lived in council-owned properties, principally on the ward's three council housing estates, namely Cantebury, Broomfields and Manchester Road.

Little Horton originally grew up around and along what is now Little Horton Lane, which rises from the city centre and heads towards Wibsey. Travelling up this road one is almost immediately struck by two impressive structures, which sit opposite one another – St Luke's Hospital and All Saints Church. The hospital was originally Bradford Union Workhouse, built in 1851–2 at a cost of £11,000. All Saints was founded and financed by Francis Sharp Powell. Construction began in 1861 and the magnificent church was consecrated in March 1864, having cost over £15,000. All Saints was intended to replace St Peter's as Bradford Cathedral, but in the end it was felt that it was too far from the city centre to fulfil this role. The church is now a Grade II listed building that remains central to the welfare of the surrounding community and in 1988 was instrumental in the founding of the Hutson Street Community Association. More recently a £2 million development known as the Landmark Centre was announced. This was intended as a place for local people of all cultures and backgrounds to meet, break down barriers, develop skills and find opportunities to make Little Horton a good place to live and work.

Tucked away behind All Saints is Little Horton Green. Its eponymous main street is steeped in the area's history, for it is here that the Sharp family, long associated with Little Horton, made their homes in two large houses – Horton Hall for the senior branch of the family, Horton Old Hall, rather confusingly, for the younger branch. The famous mathematician and astronomer, Abraham Sharp (1651–1742), once lived at Horton Hall, adding a flat-topped tower as an observation post. Sadly, both houses were demolished in the late 1960s, this being described by George Sheeran, a local architectural historian, as one of Bradford's most serious architectural losses.

Little Horton Green has lost nothing of its old charm, however, boasting several 17th-century stone houses bearing such charming names as Bluebell Cottage and Ladybird Cottage. At one end of the street stands a row of three-storey late 18th-century textile workers' cottages, originally used in the manufacture of cotton. One resident, interviewed in a local newspaper in June 2000, revealed that keys are regularly heard rattling in the door to her house – usually in the very early morning – suggesting the presence of the ghost of a watchman, or perhaps a 'knocker-upper' once employed to rouse workers for their days toil. The Powell estate still owns most of the historic houses at Little Horton Green (the exception being Little Horton Hall, privately owned and recently refurbished), the tenants paying rent to the estate, and the architectural diversity contained in this one street is perhaps unique in the district. All the properties are now Grade II listed buildings, and the whole of the green is a conservation area. There can't be many other areas like Little Horton Green in the Bradford district – a genuine ancient village surrounded by open space yet almost within the heart of the city itself. It is a huge hit with visitors to the city, and American tourists in particular have been known to take time out from their summer vacations to the area to photograph the charming scenes to be found here.

A little further up Little Horton Lane, Horton Park Avenue branches off to the right. This was where Bradford Park Avenue, Bradford's other professional football league club, played their home games until their expulsion from the league in 1970. The stadium's main stand was 'double-sided', one side facing the football pitch, the other facing a cricket ground which has been used by Yorkshire CC. After Avenue left the Football League, they moved to Bradford City's Valley Parade ground, and their former home gradually fell into a sad state of disrepair. The stands eventually came down and a sports centre was recently built on the site. Horton Park lies further along the avenue that bears its name.

Little Horton has a long tradition of welcoming people of other nationalities and cultures into its midst. After World War Two many Eastern European refugees made their home in this part of the city, and close-knit communities of Poles, Ukrainians, Hungarians and Lithuanians, among others, sprang up. The Polish community established an ex-servicemen's club in the area, as well as a Polish parish club. The community provided classes on Saturday mornings in order to teach children of Polish descent the language of their forefathers. Today Little Horton is home to many families of Asian descent, continuing the tradition of a diverse cultural mix in the area.

Little Horton is not without its problems, however. In the late 1990s the council ward of Little Horton was named in a Government Index of Deprivation as being the second most deprived and run-down ward in the entire country. The Park Lane area of the ward won a grant of £50 million from the Government's New Deal for Communities scheme, so positive steps to help alleviate the unemployment and related problems being experienced are finally being made. Project organisers intended to cut the area's 13.6 percent unemployment rate to the district average of 5.1 percent.

So, like other suburbs of Bradford, Little Horton is an area of contrasts. The poverty and deprivation of some parts of the ward stand in total contrast to the historic core of the village – Little Horton Green – an oasis of charm almost in the heart of the city.

**Further Reading**

**Cudworth, William** *Rambles Round Horton,* Thos. Brear & Co, 1886

Little Horton Green is tucked away behind All Saints' Church, May 1975. *(Jack Booth)*

The picturesque cottages and houses on Little Horton Green are popular with tourists, who love photographing them, July 1980. *(Jack Booth)*

Old Red Lion Inn, Little Horton Lane, *c.*1900. *(Bradford Libraries)*

The Old House at Home, Little Horton Lane, *c.*1900. *(Bradford Libraries)*

Horton Hall stood near to little Horton Green *c.*1900. *(Bradford Libraries)*

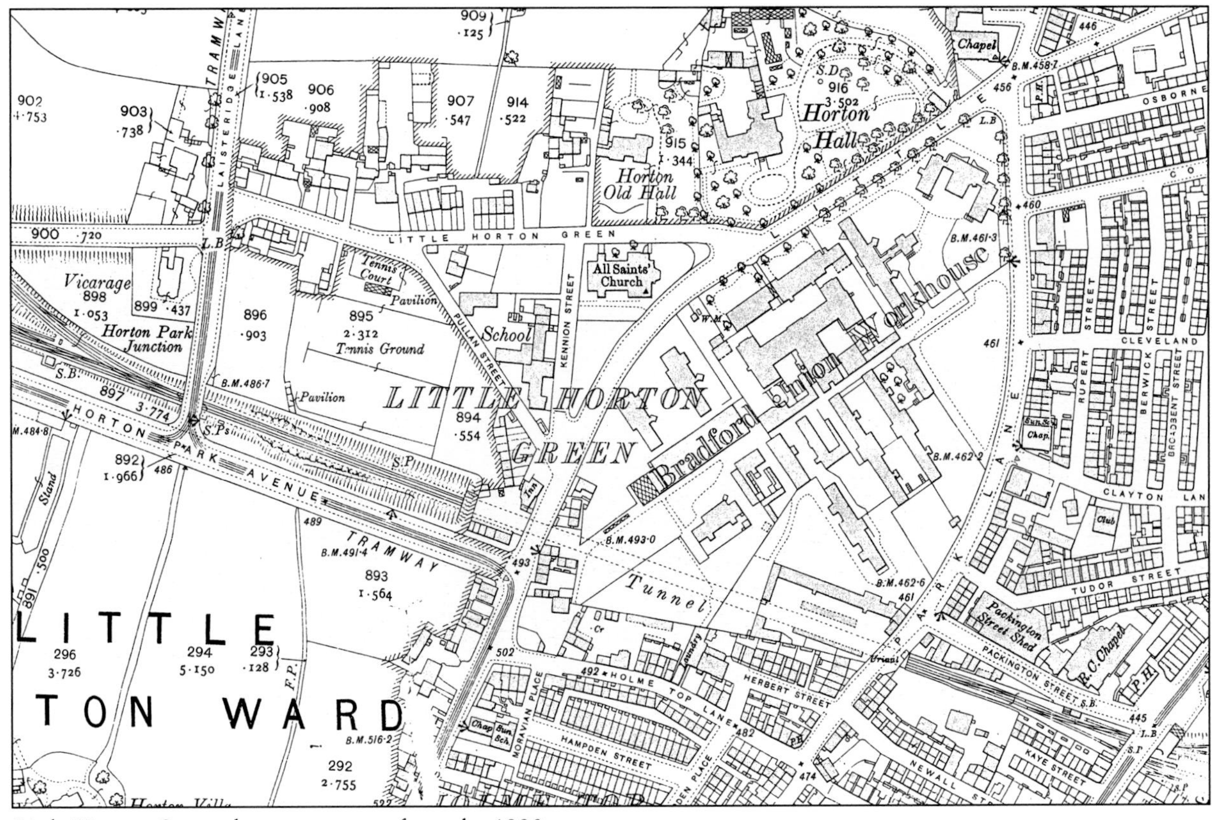


Little Horton Green shown on a map from the 1890s.

All Saints' Church, 1877. All Saints' was founded and financed by Francis Sharp Powell, construction began in 1861 and the magnificent church was consecrated in March 1864, having cost over £15,000. *(Bradford Libraries)*

This illustration of Little Horton Green appeared in the *Illustrated Weekly Telegraph*, pictured in around 1885. *(Bradford Libraries)*

Little Horton: houses to be pulled down for road widening, *c.*1900. *(Bradford Libraries)*

# Great Horton

GREAT Horton lies to the south-west of Bradford, between the inner city and the outer, rural suburbs. The modern council ward of Great Horton includes the historic village of Great Horton itself, as well as the areas of Lidget Green, Scholemoor and Paradise Green. Great Horton, along with its namesake neighbour, Little Horton, formed the ancient township of Horton, which was one of the original areas included in the Borough of Bradford at its incorporation in 1847. The ward is one of the smallest in the Bradford district, covering only 1.2 square miles. Bradford Council describes Great Horton, in its ward profile, as being diverse, having pockets of industry and commerce, housing and open space.

In ancient times Great Horton was known as Horton Magna, and seems to have developed slowly over the centuries, for as recently as the early 19th century very few houses existed there. The main road through Great Horton, the Bradford to Halifax Road, had several lanes and folds running off it, but Cudworth states that there was 'not a single street, except that formed by the "row" of houses, latterly known as "Knight's Fold"'. Detached dwellings were scattered on either side of the main road, and two large open spaces known as Great Horton Green and Upper Green were prominent. Great Horton Green included Low Fold, which was reached by Paternoster Lane, described as probably one of the oldest thoroughfares in Great Horton. By the mid-1880s both greens had been widely built on.

Family names often become synonymous with an area and become entwined in its recorded history, and in this respect Great Horton is no exception. The Blamires family, a large and well-respected family, owned many properties in Great Horton, including Blamires Farm, a homestead near Cliffe Mills. In the first few decades of the 19th century several members of the Blamires family were butchers by trade, including Samuel Blamires, who also kept the Kings Arms Inn on Great Horton Road. His brother William had a butchers shop in Kirkgate, Bradford, and was known for being 'close-fisted', apparently a family trait of the Blamires. When haggling with customers over the price of a prime joint, William would raise his skewer saying 'I don't get that at it!' The buyer would naturally assume that he meant that if he dropped his price he wouldn't be able to afford a new skewer, while in reality he was referring to the nearby Piece Hall building, which his skewer was pointing at, and which he evidently had designs on. Judging by the amount of property listed in his will (dated 1827) the skewer must have had the desired effect.

Another name that occurs regularly in records relating to Great Horton is Brooksbank. Rather confusingly, this family seem to have had something of a liking for naming their sons Gilbert, as the name appears on documents of 1602, 1675 and 1704, and the initials GB appear on several residences in Great Horton, dating from the 1730s and 1740s. Brooksbank Old Hall and the nearby Kings Arms were both built by the family.

Today, Great Horton retains many links to its past. The trip out of the city centre, up Great Horton Road, is not the most inspiring in the Bradford district, but on reaching the village, one may well be surprised just how many of the original features have survived. Delightful cottage properties, from a time when Great

Horton was truly a separate community, are dotted here and there; two of them on the main road are dated 1697. Benson Turner's mill, once the major employer in the area, is still there, now divided up into units. It must have seemed as if everyone in Great Horton worked at the mill, and the roads would have been thick with workers making their way home at the end of the day. The workers were known as 'currant cakers' after the teacakes for their lunches, which they often carried in large red handkerchiefs. The teacakes were known as the 'Great Horton Beef'.

One of Bradford's first working men's clubs opened in Great Horton in 1886. The club is known locally as the 'Fat Pot', a name that harks back to the very reasons for the club's existence. The legend goes that a group of young men would meet for drinks at the Four Ashes pub on a Sunday evening. The landlord got into the habit of providing them with bread and a jar of dripping (a fat pot) as a kind of bar snack. Eventually the landlord must have got fed up with giving free food out as he stopped the practice, much to the annoyance of the young men, who got together and decided that if the Four Ashes wasn't going to provide them with their Sunday night treat, they would have to start their own working men's club, complete with its own 'fat pot'.

Great Horton's main places of worship are St John the Evangelist Church (which is Great Horton's parish church) and the Methodist Church. Both are imposing structures, which are seen as landmarks in the area. Great Horton Library, on Cross Lane, is something of a focal point for the community and is situated in a beautiful old building, perhaps one of Bradford's finer settings for such a place of wisdom and learning.

The latter half of the 20th century brought many changes to Great Horton. Increasing traffic led to alterations and developments, although locals were relieved when the historic centre of the village was made a conservation area, preserving its character and true 'village atmosphere' for future generations. Hunt Yard, just up from the junction of Cross Lane and Great Horton Road, has something of a history attached to it. Traditionally the lands there were granted following the slaying of Bradford's famous wild boar. Hunt Yard was extensively redeveloped in the 1970s, and the Housing Development built there won two national awards for architectural merit in 1978.

The late 1980s brought something of a revival to Great Horton's sense of community when a village hall was opened on Beldon Road. The hall featured a meeting room, coffee shop and lounge, and was used by a variety of local groups of all ages and backgrounds. Falling profits led to the hall's closure in November 2001, although plans are afoot to rescue it and put it back into community use.

Great Horton became the proud owner of a village green to mark the millennium. A piece of land known locally as the Black Mountain, the site of a former quarry, woollen works and tile and brick works, was cleaned up and developed as a focal point for the community, the scheme being boosted by a £50,000 grant from the Countryside Agency. Under the nationwide Millennium Green Scheme, the land is protected from any development for 999 years.

Great Horton, then, is historically an important part of Bradford, being one half of the township incorporated in 1847. Its history is entwined with that of the city. To this day, it remains a diverse and in some ways surprising suburb of Bradford.

**Further Reading**

**CBMC Planning Division** *Great Horton* CBMC, 1976.

**Cudworth, William** *Rambles Round Horton* Thos. Brear & Co., 1886.

High Street, Great Horton *c.*1900. *(Bradford Libraries)*

Crag Lane, off Great Horton Road, in 1974. *(Jack Booth)*

Halls Old House, High Street, *c.*1900. *(Jack Booth)*

Blamires House, High Street, *c.*1900. The Blamires family, a large and well-respected family, owned many properties in Great Horton. *(Bradford Libraries)*

Hunt Yard, 1978. Hunt Yard was extensively redeveloped in the 1970s, and the housing development built there won two national awards for architectural merit in 1978. *(Jack Booth)*

Fair Becca Farm, Cliffe Lane. The ghost of 'Fair Becca', who had been murdered by her sweetheart, was said to haunt the Hew Clews area of Great Horton, *c.*1900. *(Bradford Libraries)*

# IDLE

THE township of Idle, to the north of Bradford, has always been quite large in both area and population. William Cudworth described the extent of Idle in *Round About Bradford* (1876) as reaching '...from Apperley Bridge to Windhill Bridge, and from Buck Mill to Bolton Outlanes.' The population today, due to the new housing developments that rapidly appeared from the mid-20th century onwards, is near to 10,000.

The origins of the name Idle can be the subject of much speculation. The spelling of the word in historical documents is often Idell or Ydell, and J. Horsfall Turner, the noted Bradford historian, stated that the spelling Idle was frequently used in the Calverley parish register for the best part of 300 years. Another Bradford historian, William Claridge, suggested that the village took its name from the fact that much of the locality was uncultivated moorland; land that was literally idle.

Idle is well documented through history, and indeed seems to have been settled, or at least passed through, as far back as Roman times. One William Storey, when opening a quarry on Idle Moor in around 1800, found many Roman coins, and human remains enclosed in stone were also discovered. Written records mention Idle (or, rather, Idel) as far back as the 12th century, when Nigel de Plumpton is quoted as giving a piece of land there to the nuns of Esholt. The Plumpton family are associated to quite a considerable extent with Idle's past, and Sir William Plumpton and his son and heir (also William) took part in the Battle of Towton near Tadcaster in 1461. The younger William was killed in the battle, plunging the Plumptons into years of turmoil and dispute, which eventually saw the Manor of Idle being first halved and then quartered, the portions being owned at any one time by George, Earl of Cumberland (father of Lady Anne Clifford), and Sir John Constable, who split his half between his two daughters. Possession of the manor eventually ended up in the hands of Robert Stansfield, of Bradford, who bought it in the 1750s from the Calverley family. A detailed account of this early period in Idle's history is available in Cudworth's *Round About Bradford.*

By the mid to late 19th century, Idle, like much of the Bradford district, was heavily involved in the textile industry. A look at the Ordnance Survey map of 1893 shows many mills in the area, including Castle Mills, Union Mill on Butt Lane and the nearby New Mills. By the 1870s around 1,100 people from Idle were employed in the township's mills. Idle seems to have achieved some kind of parity in the size of the mills that operated there. Cudworth states that no giant manufacturer dominated the neighbouring companies in the village. Indeed he goes on to say that the villagers of the late 19th century were probably the most 'equal' in the entire land, with no man of exalted rank or great wealth residing in the township. The villagers displayed a prominent love of their home but Cudworth found them rather 'clannish' in their attitudes to outsiders.

Another source of income and employment in 19th century Idle was quarrying. Stone was dug underground from beneath Idle Moor and raised to the surface via deep shafts, so unlike areas such as Bradford Moor with its vast coal mining operations, the landscape was not utterly ruined. Idle stone was well known and was considered superior to stone from many other areas. It was used on public buildings in many towns in England, and was even exported

The view down High Street towards the Green. *(Ann Birdsall)*

as far as China, Australia and South America. Among those involved in extracting Idle stone in the early 19th century were William Storey of nearby Apperley, William Child of Greengates, and later Thomas Denbigh, among others.

Idle grew rapidly during the 19th century, reflecting an increase in the population of the Bradford district as a whole. In 1801 the township's population had been around 3,400, yet by 1871 it had risen to over 12,000.

The world famous Idle working men's club. Honorary members have included Lester Piggott. *(M. Birdsall)*

At this time the village itself was well established, along lines that are easily recognisable today. At the top of the village, on Towngate, the Old Chapel of Ease, which was erected in 1630, was still in its original use. The chapel came by its name due to the fact that the nearest parish church was at Calverley, quite a

The Green, Idle. This is the ancient centre of the village. *(Gina Szekely)*

trek away, so the chapel was quite literally built for the ease of the people of Idle. The building currently houses the highly successful Stage 84 drama school. Adjoining the Old Chapel was the township's lock-up, complete with stocks. On the opposite side of Towngate and a little further down stands Holy Trinity Church, built in 1830. Just across from the church is the former library building, a large Victorian structure which seems to loom over the road. The rooms above the library were latterly used as meeting rooms for local clubs and societies but were once used for meetings of the Idle local board, which oversaw the township's affairs. The library moved into former shop premises in a more centralised location just below the Green in the early 1990s.

Idle can aptly be described as a village of two halves. First there is the top half, centred around High Street, which runs steeply downhill from Highfield Road to the Green, from around which the bottom half of Idle radiates. It was at the junction of Highfield Road and High Street that workmen making road improvements uncovered three ancient cellars. The discovery, in 1987, caused much excitement in the local community, and it was suggested that the cellars offered proof of the location of the old Manor House, lost to historians for many years. The proof of this theory may never now be tested as the cellars, which may have had underground passages running to Holy Trinity Church, were subsequently filled in. High Street is also home to the wonderfully named Idle working men's club. The club has found international fame due to its name and has boasted celebrities such as jockey Lester Piggott and Tom O'Connor among its honorary members.

The bottom half of the village still boasts an array of small local shops, but the lure of nearby supermarkets with their cheap prices has inevitably caused something of a decline. In its heyday Idle had its own railway station and cinema, both now long gone. The station was on the line between Laisterdyke and Windhill, which opened to passengers in April 1875. Sadly there is now little evidence left of the railway line that neatly bisected the village, reinforcing the division between upper and lower Idle.

Idle today is a busy, well-populated suburb of Bradford. Smart, early 20th century housing lines Highfield Road, and a modern complex of flats stands on Bradford Road, at its junction with Idlecroft Road. The village itself has many excellent facilities for its residents to enjoy. Small shops around the Green almost give the centre of Idle the appearance of a Dales market town. Idle boasts its fair share of pubs – the New Inn and the White Bear at the very top of the village, the Alexander and the Brewery Tap down on Albion Road, and the White Swan, which stands on the Green, to name but a few. The village has two supermarkets within easy reach, and Dunne's retailers lies close to the centre. A new medical centre was built on Highfield Road in the early 1990s, and the village has numerous clubs and societies to occupy its residents.

Like many of Bradford's other suburbs then, Idle is a popular, pleasant place to live, offering all the trappings of modern living, yet retaining something of its historic appearance and charm. This is most definitely one part of Bradford that doesn't live up to its name.

**Further Reading**

**Cudworth, William** *Round About Bradford,* 1876. (Reproduced 1968, Arthur Dobson Publishing Co.)

**Watson, W.** *Idlethorp,* 1951.

**White, E.** *Idle Folk* Idle & Thackley Heritage Group, 1995.

**White, E.** *Idle, an Industrial Village* Idle & Thackley Heritage Group, 1992.

Chapel of Ease, Towngate. This is now the home to the drama school Stage 84. *(Bradford Libraries)*

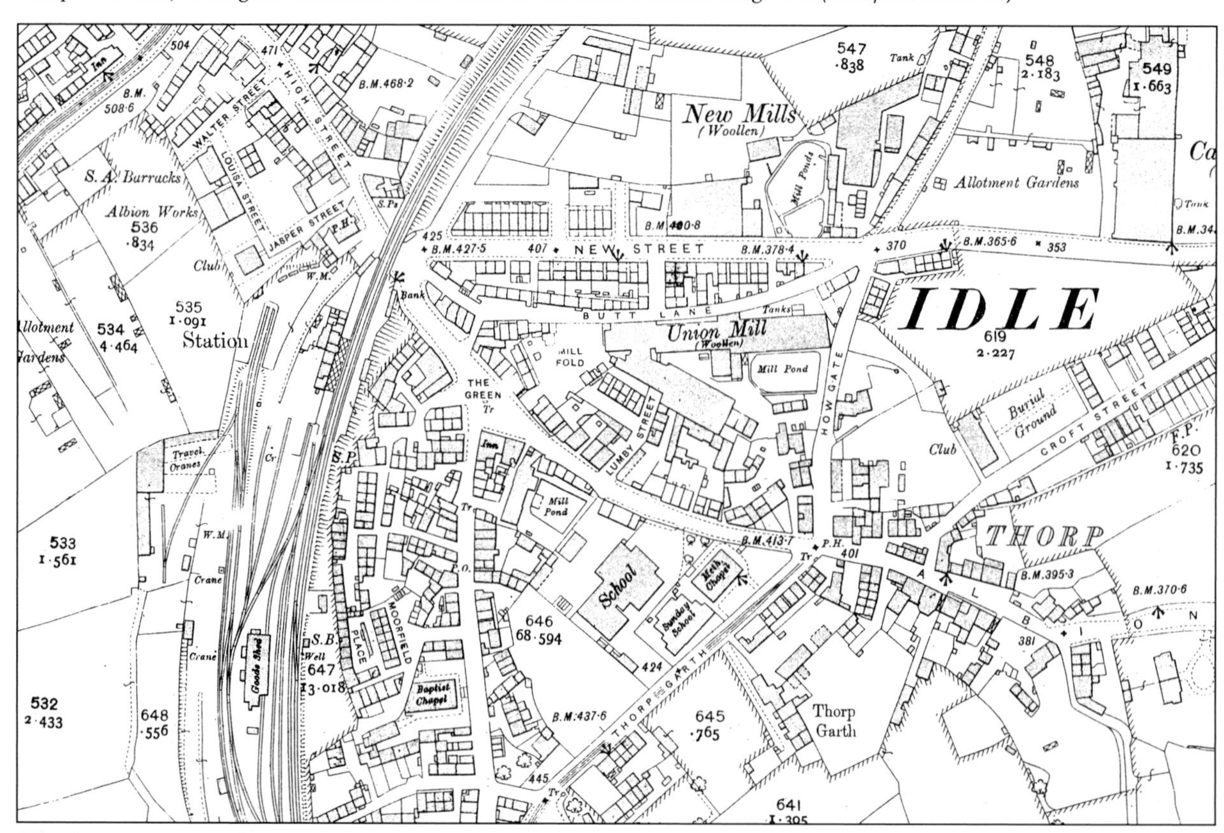


Idle shown on a map from 1908.

# LAISTERDYKE

WHAT was once the industrial village of Laisterdyke has been described in the *Telegraph & Argus* as a barometer of Bradford's fortunes, reaching a peak of activity before the war and declining thereafter with some attempt at regeneration in the 1980s and 1990s.

Its name originates from the Anglo-Saxon and means farm buildings with facilities for drainage. However, any rural identity was lost with the improvement of transport in the 19th century and the establishment of industry in the area. The old Great Northern railway line was constructed in 1854 and passed through Laisterdyke, which was the last stop before the terminus at the old Bradford Exchange Station. Sticker Lane was part of the old turnpike road, Dudley Hill to Killinghall, near Harrogate. Opposite Bar Street in Laisterdyke stood the turnpike gate, which was near the Methodist chapel. Bradford's first trolley bus also made its debut on the Laisterdyke to Dudley Hill route on 20 June 1911. It was numbered 240 and looked very like the tram cars which operated on routes around the city. 'Tracklesses', as they were locally known, last operated in Bradford in 1972.

Many of the population worked in the mills and in related local trades. There were three mills by the 1830s: Pearson's, Billingsley and Tankard's at Bradford Moor and the oldest, Roberts and Lupton's Junction Mill, by the old railway. However, the most famous mill in the area was W. & J. Whitehead (Laisterdyke) Limited. This was founded by two brothers, William and Joseph Whitehead. It moved to New Lane Mills and Greenhill Mills, Laisterdyke, in the early 1870s. By the 1880s, it was not only a topmakers, combers and spinners, but also a manufacturer, though manufacturing was later stopped to concentrate on the former processes. The firm prospered well into the middle of the 20th century and in 1958 formed a separate company, W. & J. Whitehead Exports (Laisterdyke) Ltd, to deal with the expanding export trade in tops and yarn. Until recently, it was the only mill left in the area, but sadly it too has now been closed. The receivers were called in July 2001 and reports blamed tough trading conditions, cheap imports and the US recession. In October 2001, the company was closed down with a loss of some 600 workers in total.

In *Remembering Laisterdyke*, Gina Bridgeland notes the number of people who moved to the area to find work, which is shown by birthplace records in the census returns. Housing was mainly in back-to-backs with a distinction between the 'posh' Bradford Moor end of Laisterdyke and the poorer Leeds Road end. Some houses were built by local businessmen, such as Revell the joiner, who built Revell Court near the railway bridge. There were a few larger houses, such as St Mary's vicarage and the station master's house above the cutting. In *Roundabout Laisterdyke*, local history group members reminisce about how the back-to-backs and narrow streets, snickets and middens provided an adventure playground for the children, but how the 'local bobby', knowing parents and where all the children lived, always managed to keep mischief to a minimum. Many children of Laisterdyke attended Bradford's first board school, the nearby Bowling Back Lane board school. The school was the first of eight purpose-built elementary schools built after the 1870 Education Act. On the first day, 156

The new Mosque, Killinghall Road, Laisterdyke. *(Gina Szekely)*

Laisterdyke Library and Community Centre. *(Ann Birdsall)*

Viraj Saree Centre, Leeds Road. Formerly the Yorkshire Penny Bank. *(Gina Szekely)*

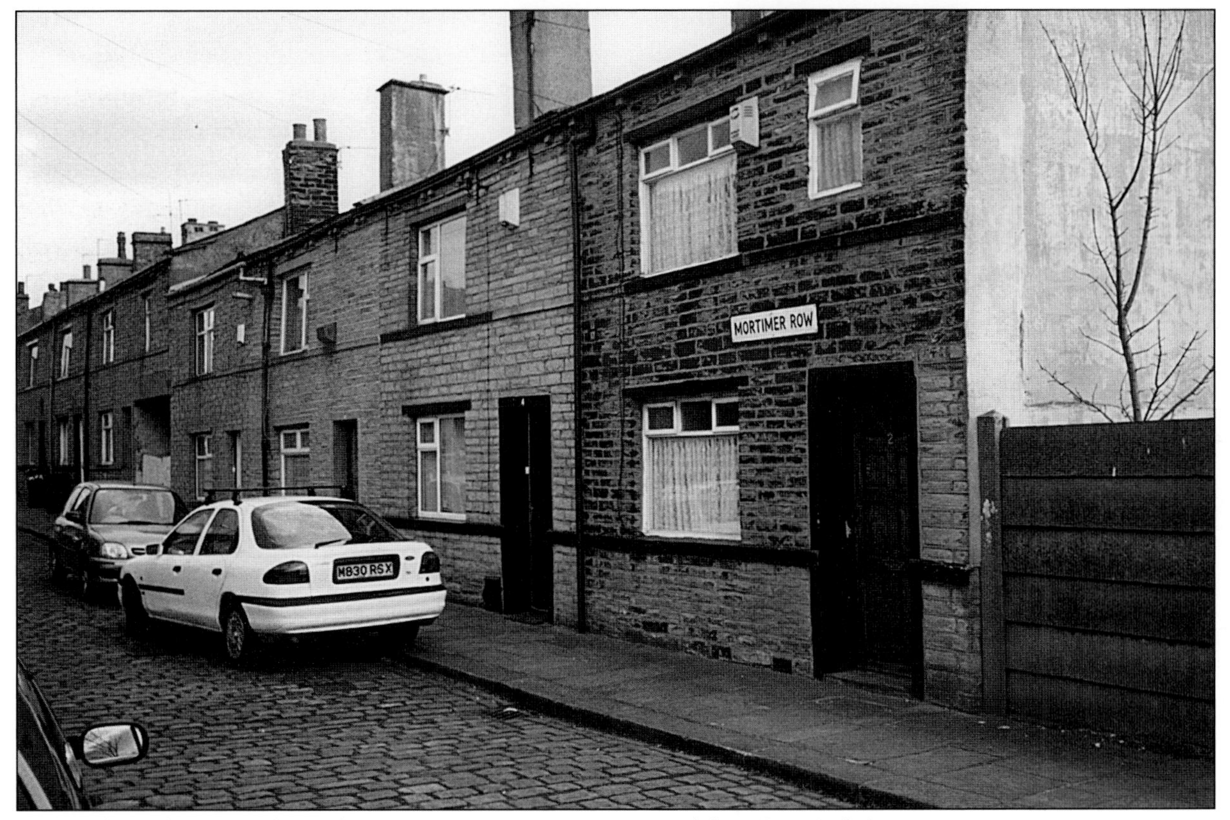


Early industrial cottages dating from 1831, Mortimer Row, Laisterdyke. *(Gina Szekely)*

pupils were admitted, but by 1886, there were 842 pupils. It has since been demolished.

To accommodate the increasing population, local retail businesses grew and before the 1940s, Laisterdyke was a busy little shopping centre from Parry Lane to Laisterdyke traffic lights, Sticker Lane. The space now occupied by Morrisons used to be a courtyard of houses and shops (Shaw's Yard). In an article for the *Bradford Star*, Dorothy Dennison recalled the once thriving centre, which not only had multiples of butchers, grocers, confectioners, newsagents and two post offices, but also a plumber, tailor, undertaker, milk dairy and herbal shop, which offered popular remedies before the National Health Service existed. Many retailers were the third or fourth generation in their family to run the business, such as Ernest Shaw, grocer in Shaw's Yard. Another grocer is also remembered, John King in Bar Street, who apparently used to 'boil' oranges to make them swell up to look larger for sale. Laisterdyke also had the Queen's Hall Cinema (opened in 1911) and a Lyceum cinema where youngsters went on a Saturday for the 'tuppeny rush' film shows.

Pubs have always maintained a presence in Laisterdyke. The Furnace Inn (1831) which sold Melbourne Ales at five old pence a pint in the 1930s survived into the 1980s. An old photograph, published in the *Telegraph & Argus* in 1984, recalls the Sunday seaside trip taken by the landlord and some of his regular customers once a year. The photo is from 1935 and shows the then landlord Tom Monaghan and his regulars in front of the motor coach especially hired for the occasion and sporting an early type of sun-roof. Apparently it was the custom for the day-trippers to throw coins to any youngsters who watched the coach leave. Halfpennies used to buy two or three ounces of boiled sweets in those days. Another pub that no longer exists, the Farm Yard pub, was kept by a Mrs Mary Butterfield in 1938. It had a summer boxing season with a ring set up in the backyard in which to hold the bouts.

Another centre of social activity is of course the local church and St Mary's is no exception. Built in 1861 down Pawson Street, it was one of 10 in a Bradford scheme to encompass a rapidly increasing population. Abednego Fold was demolished to make a site for the church. By then both Wesleyan and Primitive Methodist congregations were also active, a reflection of the growing population. St Mary's parish was constituted in July 1861. During World War Two the church was a hub of social activity when the annual pantomime continued despite shortages. The biggest event of the church year was the Bazaar, which included a pie and peas restaurant and a cinema showing silent film comedies, while the Garden Party in summer always had decorated floats for a parade around the parish. In 1988 St Mary's Church was transformed following a £50,000 refurbishment. The pulpit, pews and organ were removed, and some of the furniture was sold to an art dealer and shipped to the US, where there is great demand for such items. New carpets, lighting, heating and seating replaced the old. In 1976 Laisterdyke parish church was still at the centre of many of the area's activities, with a St John Ambulance branch, Brownies, Guides and Cubs, although unfortunately today it is almost cut off from the rest of the neighbourhood by a new factory extension. Recent years have seen the development of Laisterdyke's own Youth and Community Centre, opened in 1992. This provides courses and classes such as keep fit, and hosts parents' and toddlers' groups.

In the 1970s, Laisterdyke seemed to be slipping into dereliction and neglect. Articles in the local *Telegraph & Argus* newspaper wrote of scenes of derelict buildings and one resident described parts as in a worse condition than

St Mary's Church, Laisterdyke. *(Bradford Libraries)*

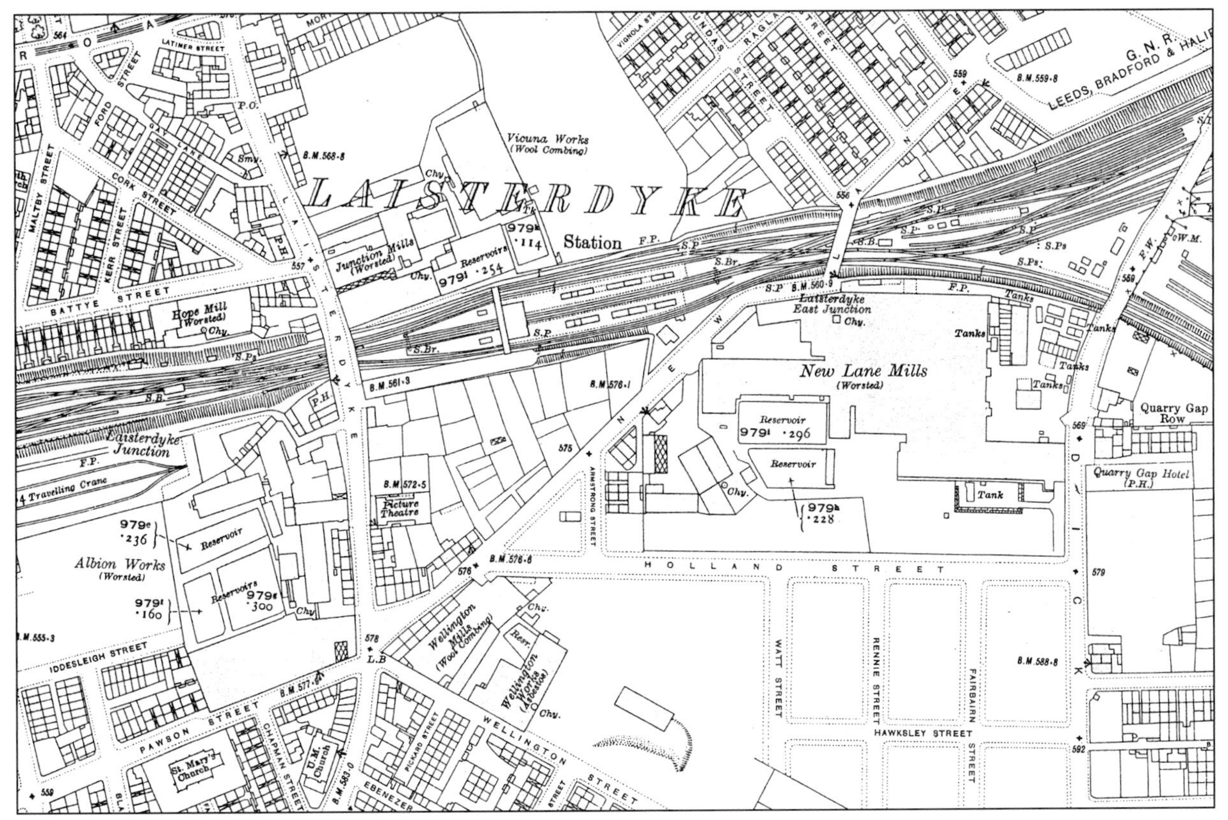


Laisterdyke shown on a map from 1921.

after the Blitz. Gone were Maltby Road, Cork Street and Gay Lane, and the old back-to-back houses were demolished as unfit. Vacant shops lined Leeds Road and land was left empty as firms sought land elsewhere in development areas. Nevertheless, some buildings were saved. Mortimer Row, dating from 1831, off Leeds Road, was spared for some modernisation as examples of early industrial cottages, following a campaign started by one of its residents, Mr Tom Wilcock. The difficulty of maintaining any village community quartered by the Bradford ring road and Leeds Road was added to by the temporary upheaval as an increasing number of Asian immigrants sought to integrate into the area.

In 2002, Laisterdyke is a busy multi-racial community with local businesses, religious buildings and community events reflecting this. The 'village' has gone forever, but Laisterdyke's new diversity adds another interesting dimension to Bradford's regional history.

Laisterdyke is also not without its famous sons and daughters. One such is Emma Sharp, famous for her feat of walking 1,000 miles in 1,000 hours at Quarry Gap, Laisterdyke. Spurred on by the failed attempt of an Australian lady in 1864 in London and her husband's doubt that any woman could perform such a task, she enlisted the support of a Mr Hardy, landlord of the Quarry Gap Hotel, Laisterdyke. She agreed to attempt the feat at the City Sporting Grounds, then attached to his house. A straight course of 120 yards was railed off for the start on 17 September, 1864. Emma walked two miles at a stretch and then rested. The walk stimulated quite a lot of interest, both day and night, and it is thought that around 100,000 people visited during the six weeks' walk, where gate money was charged. However, towards the end of the walk, a few who had betted on her not finishing tried to sabotage the walk. Emma had to have armed police guards and carry two pistols with her for the last day or two which, according to James Parker, she fired 27 times for protection, in order to finally finish her walk. On the last day, 29 October, it is reported that all the roads leading to Quarry Gap were crowded with pedestrians and vehicles of all kinds and Emma finished to cheers, the accompaniment of the Bowling Brass Band, a firework display, cannon fire and a whole sheep roasting. Emma died in 1920 at the age of 87.

A famous son of Laisterdyke is one Les Kellett, who was a genuinely tough professional wrestler, and one who, unlike today's showmen, both experienced, and probably inflicted, real injury in real fights in the 1950s, 1960s and 1970s. Saturdays are well remembered by some for dads, and indeed grandmas, yelling and wincing at the television in turn at a feast of exciting wrestling entertainment. Les Kellett was born in Laisterdyke, the son of a well-known Bradford engineer, Bill Kellett. He became generally famous as a professional wrestler when wrestling was televised in the 1960s on Saturday afternoons and he was nominated for Sports Personality of the Year in the late 1960s. He retired in 1975 and sadly died in January 2002 at the age of 86.

Should anyone wish to learn more about the history of Laisterdyke and its famous local characters, look no further than the local history group, which exemplifies the continuity of community spirit within Laisterdyke, taking a pride in its history, growth and development.

**Further Reading**

**Appleby, Jim and Jim Greenhalf** *Stories of the Century* Breedon Books Publishing Company Ltd, Derby, 1999.

**Bridgeland, Gina (ed.), with Laisterdyke Local History Group** *Laisterdyke Lives*, Bradford, 1992.

**Bridgeland, Gina (ed.), with Laisterdyke Local**

Kerr Street. Mrs Ormondroyd (in the black blouse) was born, and died, at number 32. *(Bradford Libraries)*

**History Group** *Laisterdyke Roundabout* Laisterdyke Local History Group, Bradford, 1992.

**Bridgeland, Gina (ed.), with Laisterdyke Local History Group** *Remembering Laisterdyke* University of Leeds, 1988.

**Parker, James** *Illustrated Rambles from Hipperholme to Tong* Percy Lund, Humphries & Co. Ltd, The Country Press, Bradford, 1904.

Shops between Napier Street and Thornbury Street, Laisterdyke, early 1980s. *(Bradford Libraries)*

Trolley 240 at Laisterdyke prior to setting off for Dudley Hill, 1911. *(Bradford Libraries)*

Laisterdyke toll bar. Such toll bars were very unpopular and were often the subject of attack. *(Bradford Libraries)*

# LIDGET GREEN

LIDGET Green is situated to the west of the city centre. It encompasses the area of Scholemoor. Together, their population is 6,226. Lidget, or Lidgate as it used to be known, is derived from the Saxon *hlid-geat*, meaning swing gate. Originally, there was little more than a farmstead here. It stood at a point where Bradford Road in Clayton dipped down between two low hills. Adjacent to the farmstead, and between the two hills, runs Lidget Beck. This runs northward until it joins the Bradford Beck.

One of the village's claims to fame was the support and growth of non-conformity in the area. An extract from the Quarter Session Rolls in Leeds in 1689 reads: 'An assembly of Dissenting Protestants in and about Bradford-Dale do make choice of the house of Richard Whitehouse, clerk, Lidgate near Clayton.' Lidget Green certainly played an important part, and helped spread non-conformity in the area.

One of the area's most famous sons was Dr John Fawcett. He was born in 1739 and was pastor of Wainsgate Chapel. It was one of his writings, his *Commentary on the Bible and Essay on Anger* (1802), which brought royal attention to the area. The essay was noticed by George III, who was suitably impressed with it. Fawcett refused any royal favours or recognition until an unfortunate incident in the area some time later on. A local scandal occurred concerning one of Fawcett's congregation, who was accused of forgery. Dr Fawcett wrote a letter to the king, pleading for the accused's pardon. Much to everyone's surprise, this was granted immediately.

Lidget Green was well known for its sporting traditions. There used to be three cricket grounds in the village. Indeed, Lidget Green Cricket Club was one of the earliest in the Bradford League. Bradford Rugby Union Club was also situated in the area, its home being on Scholemoor Lane. The club eventually amalgamated with Bingley and moved to that area of the city.

Lidget Green is also home to Scholemoor Cemetery. This 'forest of stone' is a tribute to Victorian extravagance, much like Undercliffe, to the north of the city.

Today Lidget Green is home to a multi-cultural society, with the largest Gujerati-Hindu community in Bradford. The area was well known for its integrated community, although recently, to the shock of the population, Lidget Green became an area of national focus after rioting. The heart of the area is the busy junction of Cemetery Road, Legrams Lane, Clayton Road and Beckside Road. Shops and restaurants abound in the area nowadays. What a far cry from the original farmstead all those years ago.

**Further Reading**

**Holgate, I.** *Lidget in Clayton* The Bradford Antiquary, New Series, Part 36, 1952.

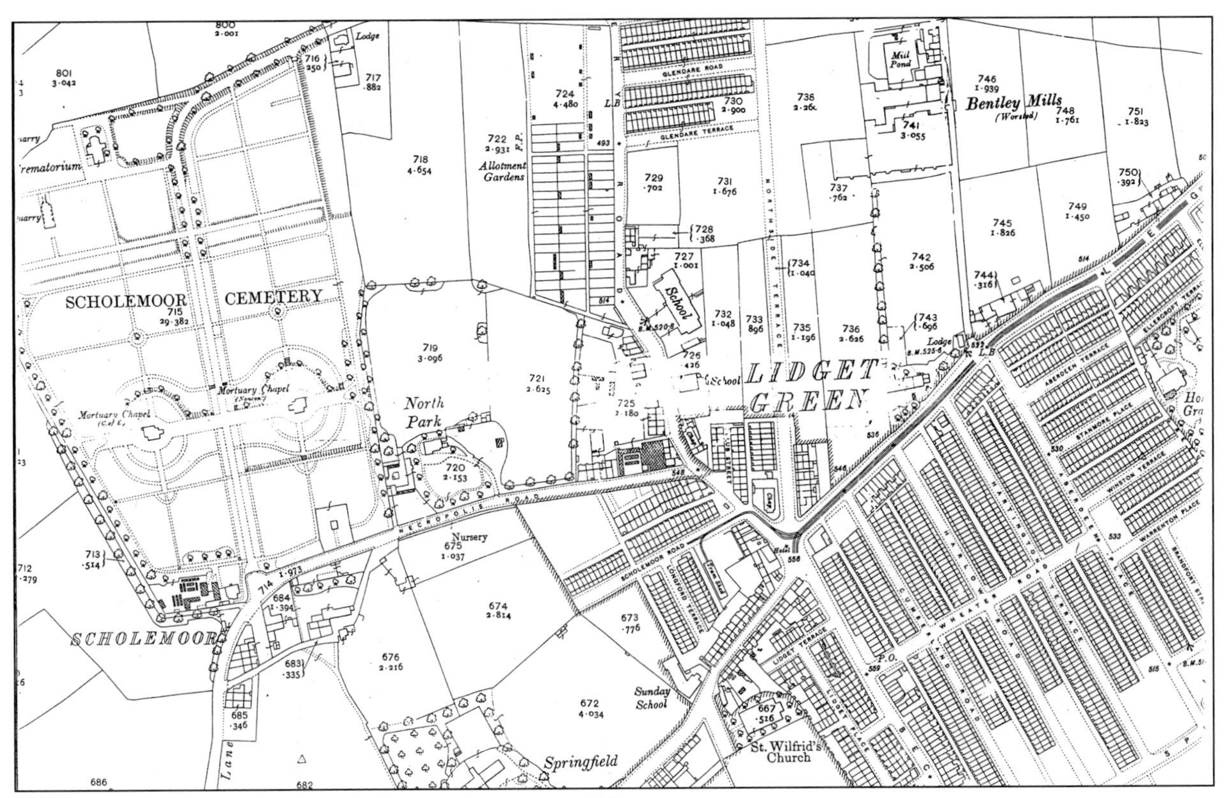


Map of Lidget Green, showing Scholemoor Cemetery, 1908.

An engraving of Scholemoor Cemetery from the *Illustrated Weekly Telegraph*, 1886.

Club Street, Lidget Green, *c.*1900. *(Bradford Libraries)*

A view of Lidget Green, taken from Pleasant Street, Great Horton. *(Jack Booth)*

# Low Moor

LOW Moor lies close to Wibsey, south of the city centre. It takes its name from its position near to the higher moorland of Wibsey and around, which once all but surrounded it. The early history of Low Moor is the story of a quiet, rural backwater with relatively few inhabitants and scattered isolated dwellings. The area had long come under the influence of the Rookes of Royds Hall, which is situated a couple of miles from Low Moor. The Rookes had made Royds Hall their home since the early 1300s, first as tenants, then from 1538 as owners of the Manor of Wibsey. The present Royds Hall dates from Elizabethan times.

During its early, rural history, Low Moor benefited from the gentle, unobtrusive influence of the Rookes family, who were essentially country squires. They farmed the land around their hall and seem to have been kind landlords who cared for their tenants. The principal forms of trade in Low Moor at that time were sheep farming and hand-loom weaving. The weavers took their wares to nearby Halifax, presumably to the Piece Hall. The village of Low Moor in the 17th and early 18th centuries has been described as a drowsy little hamlet with few cottages dotted around.

In 1606 William Rookes and one Richard Richardson of Bierley Hall obtained permission from the Archbishop of York to build a Chapel of Ease at Low Moor. Until then the area was only served by Bradford parish church, quite a considerable distance away, so the chapel was to be built for the ease of worshippers who would no longer face a lengthy return trek to Bradford. Permission was granted in 1636 for weddings, baptisms and burials to take place at the chapel, which was dedicated to the Holy Trinity. The chapel was originally known as Wibsey Chapel, only relatively recently changing its name officially to Holy Trinity.

Low Moor was changed forever in 1791 with the opening of the Low Moor Ironworks. The four men responsible for setting up the company behind the works were John Hardy, a solicitor, Revd Joseph Dawson of Idle, a Mr Hird, a woolstapler, and a Mr Jarrett, a draper. The four had purchased the land in 1789. Almost as soon as the ironworks were opened the development of the Low Moor area began. In the same way that the nearby Bowling Ironworks transformed that township, so the landscape of Low Moor was altered almost beyond recognition. Houses went up at an alarming rate to accommodate the hundreds of workers employed at the site. The company went on to build schools for the workers' children and other such facilities, and the partners seem to have regarded themselves as the new lords of the manor, and tried to live up to the example set by successive generations of Rookes. The iron produced at Low Moor became famous, and the works turned out products such as wagon wheels, rails and, increasingly, weaponry such as cannons, shot and rifle parts. Pictures and engravings of the ironworks show countless chimneys belching thick smoke, furnaces and heaps of spoil creating a scene which almost resembles something out of a nightmare. Indeed, conditions in and around Low Moor as a whole must have been harsh when the works were at the height of their productivity.

So during the 19th century Low Moor had been completely transformed from its sleepy, rural roots to a built-up industrial area. The population of the district had rocketed – the ironworks alone employed around 3,500

A general view of Low Moor taken in around 1906. *(Bradford Libraries)*

Scott's School, Low Moor. John Scott, then his son, were headmasters here for 62 years from 1838. *(Bradford Libraries)*

people in its heyday, and the area could boast many new amenities for its inhabitants such as schools, chapels and shops. Central School was built in 1814, and came to be known as Scott's School after John Scott, and later his son, who were headmasters at the school for a total of 62 years from 1838. New Works School, which later became Low Moor Girls' School, was built in 1872, and Hill Top School in 1843. The recreational as well as the educational needs of the community were amply provided for at Harold Park. This 21-acre site was opened in 1885, and named after the Hon. Harold Hardy, a son of the Earl of Cranbrook and former manager of the Low Moor Company. The park became the recreational centre of Low Moor with tennis courts, gardens and a boating lake. The Harold Park Carnival was a much-loved yearly event with bands, a procession and even swimming competitions in the lake. The Harold Club on Huddersfield Road was opened in 1883. Facilities for its members were excellent – bowling teams, games, a library and even a bathroom complete with a bath which members were charged 1d to use. The Harold Club celebrated its centenary in 1983 and continues to this day.

The railway system reached Low Moor in July 1849 with the opening of the line to Cleckheaton. A branch to Halifax opened the following month and following the completion of the Bowling tunnel, Low Moor was connected to Bradford by rail. Low Moor became something of a rail centre, with the building in 1864 of sheds, which could house up to 75 engines. Houses were built nearby for the drivers, firemen and their families. Not surprisingly the houses became known as Railway Terrace.

Perhaps not all the trappings of modern life arrived in Low Moor as quickly as in other areas, however, if one is to believe a tale related by William Cudworth. Seemingly a pocket watch, which must have been accidentally dropped outdoors, was found by some locals who didn't know what this strange 'clicking-thing' was. A particularly respected 'Low Moorite' known as Wise Willie, was summoned to shed light on matters. After studying the watch carefully he admitted that while he didn't know exactly what this strange object was, it was probably 'some mak ov a toad'! The watch was buried, presumably on Wise Willy's advice, to prevent it causing any mischief.

During the 20th century Low Moor went into a steady decline. The ironworks hit a recession, changing hands repeatedly before ceasing production at the site completely in the 1950s. The area's other main employer – its chemical works – was rocked by a massive explosion on 21 August 1916. Thirty-nine people were killed at the plant and 60 injured following an outbreak of fire which led to the explosions. It was wartime however, and so strong were the restrictions on reporting such incidents that Low Moor was not named as the site of the explosion in any of the contemporary newspaper reports. Six firemen were among the dead, and workers who survived fled the disaster scene with their hair bleached blond and their skin stained yellow by the chemicals in the smoke. Extensive damage was caused in Low Moor, with windows smashed and houses left with their roofs blown off. A monument to the dead firemen was later erected in nearby Scholemoor Cemetery.

The 1960s and 1970s saw a great deal of change in Low Moor. Development was taking place on a vast scale across much of the Bradford district, with old properties being demolished, new housing estates appearing and road-widening schemes being carried out to improve transport. In Low Moor various fine buildings, some of which had been built for the community by the Low Moor Company, began to disappear. The original vicarage for the Holy

Old Park House, Low Moor, *c.*1900. *(Bradford Libraries)*

Trinity Church was demolished in 1964, its site being covered by the Park House Estate. Low Moor station closed to passengers in June 1965, lasting for another year as a goods station before being closed completely. There was a general feeling of neglect in parts of Low Moor when streets were emptied of their residents, the houses then being left to await demolition. Vandals, squatters and even gypsies quickly moved in to replace the residents and angry locals demanded action from the council. The matter made it into the pages of the *Telegraph & Argus* in 1972 with one resident saying that Low Moor used to be one of the nicest villages in the area, while the council replied that as quickly as they boarded the houses up, vandals broke in again.

Eventually the programme of demolition was completed and new housing and shops were built, including some British Legion sheltered flats, named after Mr Avery Tulip, a well known member of the local community. Today Low Moor is a vibrant suburb of Bradford. Ciba, formerly Allied Colloids chemical works, has its home in the area, continuing the long history of industry. The Harold Club and Harold Park still exist and serve the community well, as well as providing a link to Low Moor's historic past.

An excellent account of growing up in the Low Moor area was published in 1996. *Low Moor ...the beginning of a Journey* by Norman Ellis gives a wonderful, personal insight into the characters, businesses and social life of Low Moor, written by one who lived in the area all his life.

The ever-popular Harold Club, Low Moor, pictured in around 1900. *(Bradford Libraries)*

**Further Reading**

**Cudworth, William** *Round About Bradford,* 1876 (Reproduced 1968, Arthur Dobson Publishing Co.)

**Ellis, Norman** *Low Moor ...the beginning of a Journey* Low Moor Local History Group, 1996.

**Forster Society** *Low Moor*, 1972.

**Lingard, D., C. Nicoll and J. Nicoll** *Low Moor in Times Past* Countryside publications, 1983.

The railway system reached Low Moor in July 1849 with the opening of the line to Cleckheaton. A branch to Halifax opened the following month and following the completion of the Bowling tunnel, Low Moor was connected to Bradford by rail. This view dates from April 1972. *(Jack Booth)*

Low Moor station. *(Bradford Libraries)*

A general view of the Low Moor area, taken in April 1972. *(Jack Booth)*

Permission to build a Chapel of Ease in Low Moor was granted in 1606. Originally called Wibsey Chapel it is now known as Holy Trinity Church, and is pictured here in August 1904. *(Bradford Libraries)*

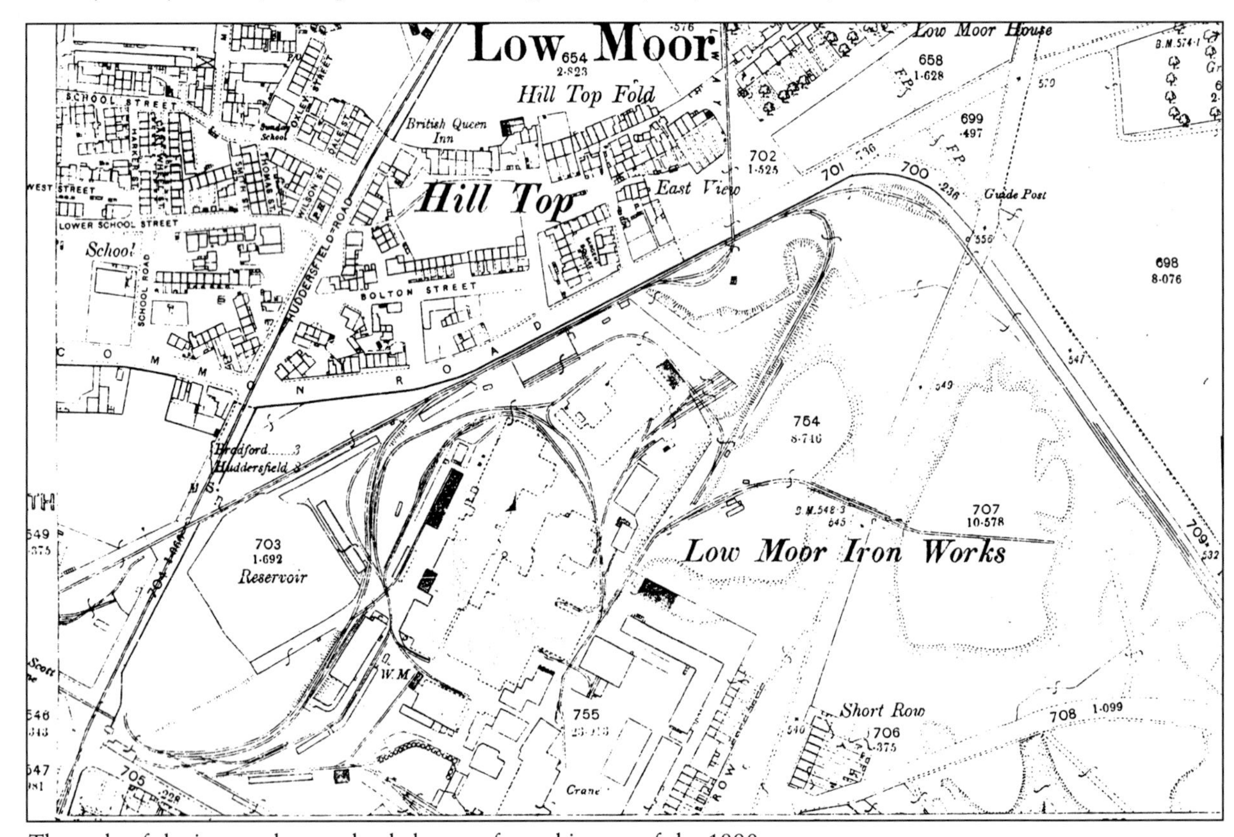


The scale of the ironworks can clearly be seen from this map of the 1890s.

# MANNINGHAM

MANNINGHAM does not appear in the Domesday Book. Bradford Dale was divided into a number of manors and had six berewicks (corn-producing lands). C. Richardson believes that these could have included Manningham and the Hortons, since their place names appear in records dating from shortly after the Domesday Book. Manningham has an early, old English form of name, because of its ending -ham. William Cudworth concentrates on 'ing' for its Norse origin and believes Manningham means the home of the son of Mann, which has great tribal associations.

Manningham was farmed according to the mediaeval communal farming system, in narrow strips in great fields. The pattern of settlement was of manorial centres surrounded by a system of great fields. The eastern boundary of the main field in which Manningham village was situated, C. Richardson shows, corresponds to Manningham Lane. He also shows that 19th-century terraced houses follow the lines of the ancient strips, probably because as fields were sold off piece by piece to builders, they were obliged to follow the lines of the ancient system.

The oldest inhabited parts of Manningham were Skinner Lane, Church Street and East Squire Lane, next to Manningham Old Hall. The highway to Keighley, which superseded the old coach road over Cottingley Moor, was completed in the 1820s, starting from the Spotted House Inn. Formerly the road from Bradford came through Frizinghall, was called Manningham Low Lane, and was described at best as a country lane lined by hedgerows.

The population increase of Bradford by about 53 percent in 1831–41 meant that the central urban area grew outwards, joining with Manningham by 1873. Manningham underwent its major growth between 1860 and 1880, with the beginning of a public transport system. Many houses had their origins in building clubs or societies, forerunners to the modern equivalent. The Oak House estate, for example, had several building societies, hence the variation in styles. After 1860 back-to-backs had to be constructed with certain spatial conditions, and they were prohibited after 1873 and replaced by terraces for working-class housing. Many of the terraces which remain in Manningham today are either post-1860 back-to-backs or post-1873 terraces, many concentrated around Manningham Mills and Drummond Mills.

The working-class suburbs however, were mainly concentrated in Bowling and the Hortons, so Manningham was the wealthier suburb. William Cudworth notes that in 1839 its rateable value was £9,503, in 1868 £61,000, and in 1895 £205,000. At the beginning of the century the residences of influential inhabitants numbered about a dozen, and by the second half of the century, Manningham had become an important suburb of Bradford for those families of influence and wealth wishing to escape Bradford's growing industrial centre. Fine Victorian terraces such as Salem Street, Manor Row (1850s) and Belle Vue Place (1839) were occupied by the middle classes, as were the elegant squares such as Hanover Square, which in 1901 was the home of Margaret MacMillan, the pioneering educationalist, and Edward Appleton, Nobel Prize-winner for physics in 1947.

Areas such as Manningham Lane, St Paul's Road, Spring Bank, Wilmer Road and Oak Lane were occupied by Bradford's merchant and professional classes. Manningham was also the site of some of Bradford's best architectural practices, such as Thomas Campbell Hope and Lockwood and Mawson. Throughout the 19th century there is evidence of a range of villa styles from neoclassical (Bolton Royd) through to Italian influence, Gothic (Oak Avenue) and Arts and Crafts (Park Road). Many of Bradford's first entrepreneurs settled in Manningham, building large houses such as Manningham Lodge and Bolton Royd (about 1832). Bolton Royd and Hallfield House (now First Church of Christ Scientist) remain, but are no longer private residences. As George Sheeran shows, both buildings show the Greek influence with Greek Doric porticoes to their main entrances. Sadly, other buildings such as Manningham Lodge have long since gone. Manningham Old Hall remains in part, however, and is currently being renovated to become a mediaeval banqueting centre. The Grade II listed building dates back to the reign of Henry VIII and massive oak beams, stone fireplaces, a 16th-century priest hole and an underground tunnel have been revealed.

In the early part of the 19th century, there was no central place of worship in Manningham and Manningham Mill was the only factory in the township which had much open ground. By the 1890s it had many places of worship, including St Jude's and St Paul's, as well as factories and dyeworks, but it was still largely residential, comprising the north-western suburbs of the city. The township made up one of the eight wards of the Borough and as a railway centre was of leading importance in the Midland Railway Company's system.

Compared to areas such as Great and Little Horton, Manningham's hand-loom weavers were few in number, only about 200, in the 1830s. In 1837, however, Mr Ellis Cunliffe Lister, MP for Bradford, built Manningham Mills, off Heaton Road, also known as Lister's Mill, for his sons John Cunliffe Lister (Kay) and Samuel Cunliffe Lister (later Lord Masham). S.C. Lister's efforts, and those of his business associates, to develop appliances for wool-combing machinery, led to the later expansion of that process into the West Riding, France and Germany. After John Cunliffe Lister's retirement, the estate passed into the sole hands of S.C. Lister in 1869, but after the mill was burned down in a fire in 1871, he went on to build the most famous Lister's Mill and it was there that he perfected the manufacture of spun silk from silk waste and thus a new branch of manufacture. According to Cudworth, Lister was 10 years researching this and wrote off a quarter of a million pounds before he began to see any profit.

Lister's (also Manningham) Mills, built in 1873, covers about 12 acres, with a massive chimney 250ft high. It is modelled on the Venetian campanile in the Piazza San Marco and upon its completion, so the story goes, the entire board of Lister & Co. were entertained to dinner in a room at the top of the stack. In its time the mill produced three times the total horse power of all other factories in Bradford and in 1890 employed 5,000 people. This imposing structure dominates the Bradford valley, not just for its former production and great industrial Italianate architecture, but also because other events there in the 1880s led to the foundation of the ILP. Following what was viewed as an unnecessary cut in wages and a refusal to negotiate, the workers went on strike. It lasted from 17 December 1890 until 27 April 1891, when it ended in defeat. During the strike the union of the Liberals and Conservatives against the strikers contributed to the trades unionists' break with those parties and the formation of the Independent Labour political organisation.

Today Lister's Mill is sadly more famous for

vandalism and dereliction over the years than for any product or project worthy of this wonderful Grade II listed building. However, it is now in the hands of the developers, Urban Splash, who hope to transform it into an £18 million residential and office complex which could also revitalise the surrounding area.

The Listers were a long-standing family in Manningham, holding land there since the middle ages. At one time the Spotted House (also called the Lister's Arms, in around 1837) was owned by S.C. Lister; part of it was used by his father, a magistrate, as a justice's room to try offenders. It was one of the oldest licensed houses in Bradford, with a name relating to the 'House at the spot' mentioned during Henry VIII's reign in 1504. At one time it had a bowling green, tennis courts and swimming pool, as well as the custom of J.B. Priestley, who was born locally in Mannheim Road and whose father Jonathan was headmaster of the local Green Lane school when it pioneered the first school meals in the country to be provided by a local authority.

Manningham Hall was built in around 1770, on the site of a previous old hall. It was brick with stone dressings and was added to by Lord Masham during his residence there. In July 1821, Parker notes that the house was struck by lightning, which passed through the dining room where about 30 people were sitting. Remarkably, injuries were slight, bar one poor servant girl whose arm was badly scorched. Lord Masham later moved to Farfield Hall, near Addingham, the ancient residence of the Cunliffe family. He offered the hall and park (which included deer at one time) to the Corporation, at £20,000 less than its value, as a gift to the public in 1870. Thereafter, the park became known as Lister Park in his honour and a marble statue was erected by public subscription in May 1875. For a while Manningham Hall was used as a restaurant before being demolished in around 1900 and replaced with Cartwright Hall art gallery, which Lord Masham also contributed towards. The hall was built of stone from the Idle Moor quarries and stands foursquare on the old engine stones from Lister's Mill. It was dedicated to Doctor Edmund Cartwright (1743–1823), in recognition of his invention of the power loom and combing machine and was felt to be more fitting for Bradford's growing civic status than the art museum then used in Darley Street. The architects were chosen by competition (117 entries) in 1899. J.W. Simpson and E.J. Milner Allen of London, who had worked on Glasgow's Kelvingrove Galleries, were chosen; shortly after Allen retired. This fine Baroque revival building was opened in April 1904 by Lord Masham, after which there was a large banquet held at the Great Northern (Victoria Hotel, Bradford). The menu is in James Parker's book. In May of the same year, the Prince and Princess of Wales visited Bradford to open the inaugural exhibition of the hall, celebrating both art and industry. Bradford by this time had its own art club, the Arcadian, whose president was the acclaimed artist Henry La Thangue, and many local industrialists, such as Abraham Mitchel, had become art collectors and patrons.

About 10 Bradford firms exhibited their fabrics. As in the Paris Exposition, there was a fine art section, an industrial section including textiles and machinery, and a women's section celebrating arts and crafts, education and domestic science. Among other attractions were a living Somali village, a palace of illusions, a crystal maze, petrol launches and gondolas on the lake, grand illuminations and fireworks. In 1915, a very popular open-air swimming pool, the Lido, was opened, and a fair was held each August. Lister Park also contributed to the war effort when Land Girls were employed to grow vegetables in the greenhouses and flower beds.

Part of the Mughal water garden, which includes fountains, Lister Park, Manningham. *(Gina Szekely)*

Bolton Royd (*c.*1832), with its Greek Doric portico to the main entrance, was once one of the grand villas of Manningham. It is now a college. *(Gina Szekely)*

The park has since played host to the ground-breaking Mela and most recently has undergone a £4 million restoration, including a renewed boating lake, a bandstand, an adventure playground and an Indian Mughal water garden – the first of its type in Britain. The park continues to be well used by the local population and now has its own preservation group which aims to involve young people in the future of the park.

Among an active display programme, which included exhibits from the antiquities and natural history collections, Cartwright Hall held annual spring exhibitions, featuring the best in contemporary art. Later the British International Print Biennales were held there, and since its specialisation in fine art after 1974, the gallery has ventured into digital art and hosted a number of fine international exhibitions, with specialist contributions from South Asia. In 2002 it hosts a stunning exhibition of Indian silver jewellery touring the UK for the first time.

The Lister family also at one time owned the Clockhouse Estate. It did not have that name originally. Clockhouse, William Cudworth speculates, could have originated from the appearance of the first-ever clock in this part of the country and its establishment at the mansion in Manningham. In fact there was a clock in the south front of the house, enabling passers-by to see the time from the highway to Otley. A photograph shows this in Cudworth's book. At the time, in the 17th century, the property was in the hands of the Lister family. Later the property became known for the famous 'Clockhouse Case' which involved legal disputes regarding various claims to ownership. The estate was also host to Bradford's first ever sighting of an aeroplane, when aviator Gustav Hamel made an exhibition flight in his Blériot monoplane during the Bradford holiday week of 1913.

Other leisure pursuits have also made their mark in Manningham. Its famous lane has been home to the Theatre Royal, which saw Sir Henry Irving's last performance in *Becket* in 1905 and also Bradford's first Rolarena, opened in November 1908 to produce first-rate figure skaters, dancers and speed skaters. Most notably, Valley Parade, off Manningham Lane, is the home of Bradford City Football Club. Bradford City won the FA Cup in 1911 and in 1999 saw promotion to the Premier League with a victory parade through Manningham to Centenary Square. There is a monument outside the main stand to the 56 supporters who tragically lost their lives in the fire disaster of 1985.

Bradford is well known as a cosmopolitan city and, as the wealthier sectors of the community moved even further away from Bradford's centre, so the inner-city suburbs, such as Manningham, came to be the home of a variety of immigrants. Irish, Germans, Poles, Jews (from Germany, Poland and Russia), Hungarians, Ukrainians, Italians and, more recently, South Asians have all become part of Manningham's growing community over the years. Evidence is shown from the Victorian villas of Manningham, many of them built for the wealthier German merchant community in areas such as Oak Lane, St Paul's Road, the Jewish Synagogue in Bowland Street, the Catholic churches, schools and more recently mosques, Asian shops and restaurants. Frederick Delius was born in Claremont in 1862 to a German wool merchant and educated at Bradford Grammar School. Sir William Rothenstein was born in Manningham in 1872, artist and tutor of Sir Henry Moore.

Bradford's Heritage Recording unit, begun in the 1980s, has provided a wealth of invaluable information on the experiences of such immigration and integration. Its book, *Here to Stay*, (1994), covers the experience of South

Asians and includes photographs taken at the Belle Vue Studio (1902–75), also known as Sandford Taylor's, on Manningham Lane, at which photographs could be obtained to send to relatives abroad.

All these citizens have contributed to the expanding cultural life of Manningham and to the city as a whole. Manningham provided Bradford's first German lord mayor, Charles Semon, in 1864 and St George's Hall was built with the support of German merchants. Bradford is well known for its excellent Asian cuisine, and one of the first curry houses, the Sweet Centre, was established in Lumb Lane. The first Bradford Mela, which now attracts people from all over the country and is a showcase for local multiculture and commerce, was held in Lister Park.

As wealthier families sought to move even further away from Bradford centre from the late 1800s onwards, many of Manningham's larger villas, with their expensive maintenance costs, have been converted to flats and bedsits. Its older terraces have become home to South Asian families, many of whom were employed in the local textile firms – Lund Humphries, Lister's and Drummonds. Today pockets of Manningham, as in other areas of Bradford, reflect the decline in Bradford's textile and manufacturing industries, lack of local business investment and competition for local shops from larger supermarkets. Areas have become rundown, with problems of high unemployment, prostitution and drug dealing, which are always keenly felt with frustration by any surrounding communities trying to cultivate good family values, educational and economic progress. It is unfortunate then, that given such decline, Manningham should also have been the scene of rioting in June 1995, and again in July 2001, by many of the younger generations of some South Asian citizens. Sadly these riots have only served to exacerbate the problems of cultural integration, misunderstanding and decline in the local economy, which a minority believed would be better highlighted, and subsequently addressed, by such widely reported activity. It has also sadly undermined the very successful assimilation and economic regeneration undergone by the many within local communities whose origins are immigrant.

Nevertheless, there is hope for the future and for continued regeneration in the area. Manningham once again has the potential to become a dynamic suburb of Bradford, lying as it does between the city and now the newly designated world heritage site of Saltaire. Youth projects, such as the Bradford Youth Development Partnership and the new youth link between the equally disadvantaged area of Holme Wood, will help. The new £14 million challenge college nearby will hopefully prove as innovative educationally and socially as Manningham's Green Lane School did when it provided school meals for the first time. The Carlisle Business Centre continues to provide training and expertise and the large sports centre and community and youth centres are still well used. A multi-million pound regeneration package, focusing on training, education and jobs, based on an award from the Government's Single Generation Budget, aimed at Manningham and Girlington, is also underway. Hopefully, with patience, enterprise and continued investment from all, Manningham will once again become a thriving suburb, with Lister's Mill at its heart, and with a vibrant sense of progress happening.

**Further Reading**

**Appleby, Jim and Jim Greenhalf** *Stories of the Century* Breedon Books Publishing Company Limited, Derby, 1999.

*Bradford, A Centenary City* City of Bradford MDC, 1997.

**Bradford Art Galleries** *The Connoisseur, Art*

Horse-drawn tram number 64 stands at the Lister Park terminus. *(Bradford Libraries)*

*Patrons and Collectors in Victorian Bradford* Bradford Art Galleries and Museums, Bradford, 1989.

**Bradford Heritage Recording Unit** *Here to Stay, Bradford South Asian Communities* City of Bradford MC, Arts, Museums and Libraries, Bradford, 1994.

**Cudworth, William** *Histories of Manningham, Heaton, and Allerton* W. Cudworth, Bradford, 1896.

**Fieldhouse, Joseph** *Bradford* Watmoughs Limited & City of Bradford MC, Libraries Division, 1981.

**Firth, Gary** *Bygone Bradford, The 'Lost World' of J.B. Priestley* Dalesman Books, Lancaster, 1986.

**James, David** *Bradford* Ryburn Publishing Limited, Halifax, 1990.

**Parker, James** *Illustrated Rambles from Hipperholme to Tong* Percy Lund, Humphries & Co. Ltd., The Country Press, Bradford, 1904.

**Richardson, C.** *A Geography of Bradford* University of Bradford, 1976.

**Scruton, William** *Pen and Pencil Pictures of Old Bradford* The Amethyst Press, Bradford (first ed. 1890) 1985.

**Sheeran, George** *Good Houses Built of Stone* Allanwood Press Ltd, Pudsey, 1986.

**Sheeran, George** *The Victorian Houses of Bradford* Bradford Libraries and Information Service, Bradford, 1990.

**Shutt, Peter** *The Glory of Lister Park: A Century of Enjoyment' in Bob Duckett (ed.), Aspects of Bradford 2* Wharncliffe Books, 95-108, Barnsley 2000.

**Waterson, Edward and Peter Meadows** *Lost Houses of the West Riding* Jill Raines, York, 1998.

**Wright, D.G. and J.A. Jowitt (eds)** *Victorian Bradford* City of Bradford MC, Libraries Division, 1981.

Once the biggest silk mill in the world, Lister's Mill still dominates the Bradford skyline. *(Ann Birdsall)*

Lister's Mill and Valley Parade, home of Bradford City, both seem to tower above Manningham, dominating its skyline. *(Ann Birdsall)*

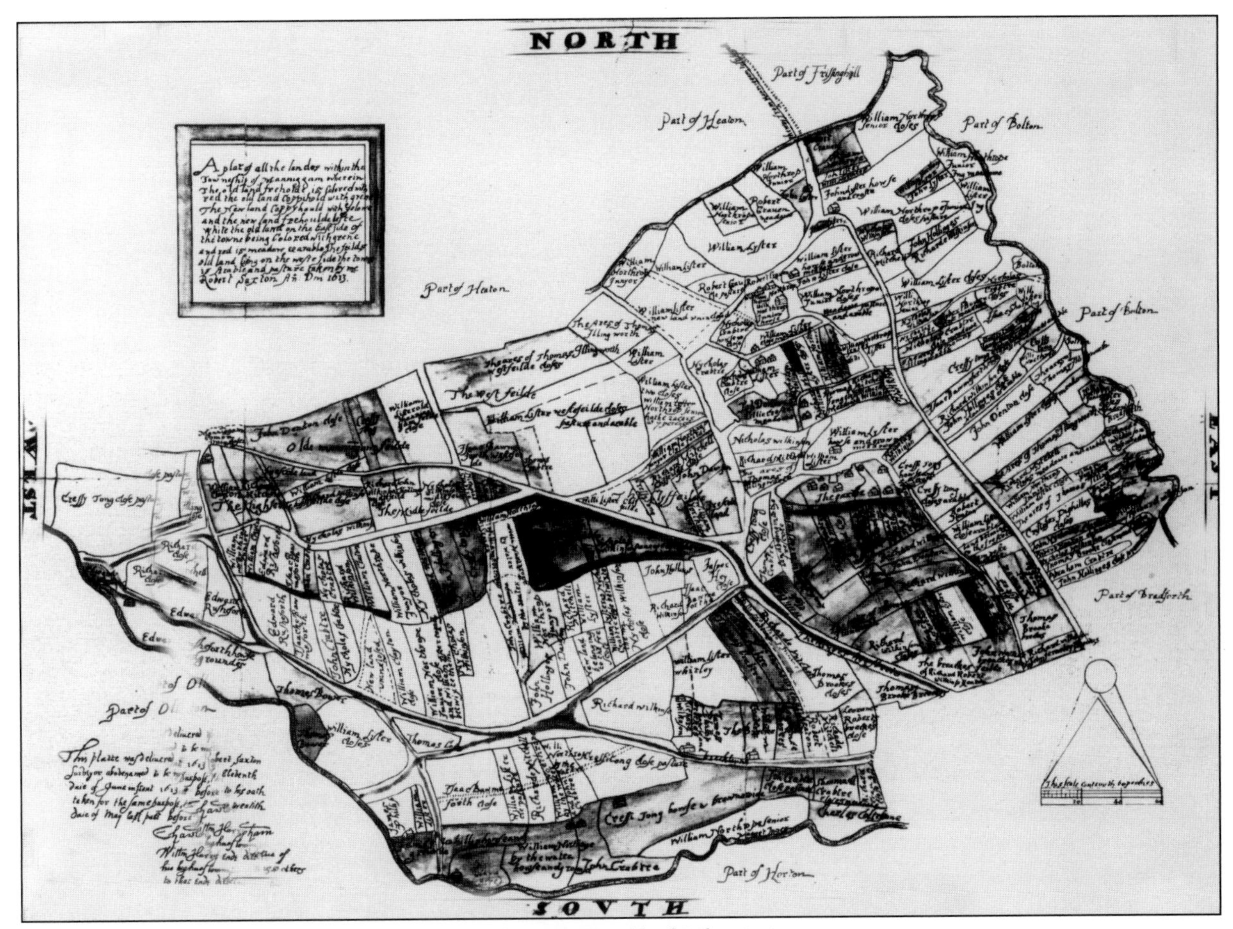


A map of Manningham by Robert Saxton, dated 1613. *(Bradford Libraries)*

Manningham (Lister's) park, from *Brear's Guide to Bradford*, 1873. *(Bradford Libraries)*

The Spotted House, Manningham Lane. *(Bradford Libraries)*

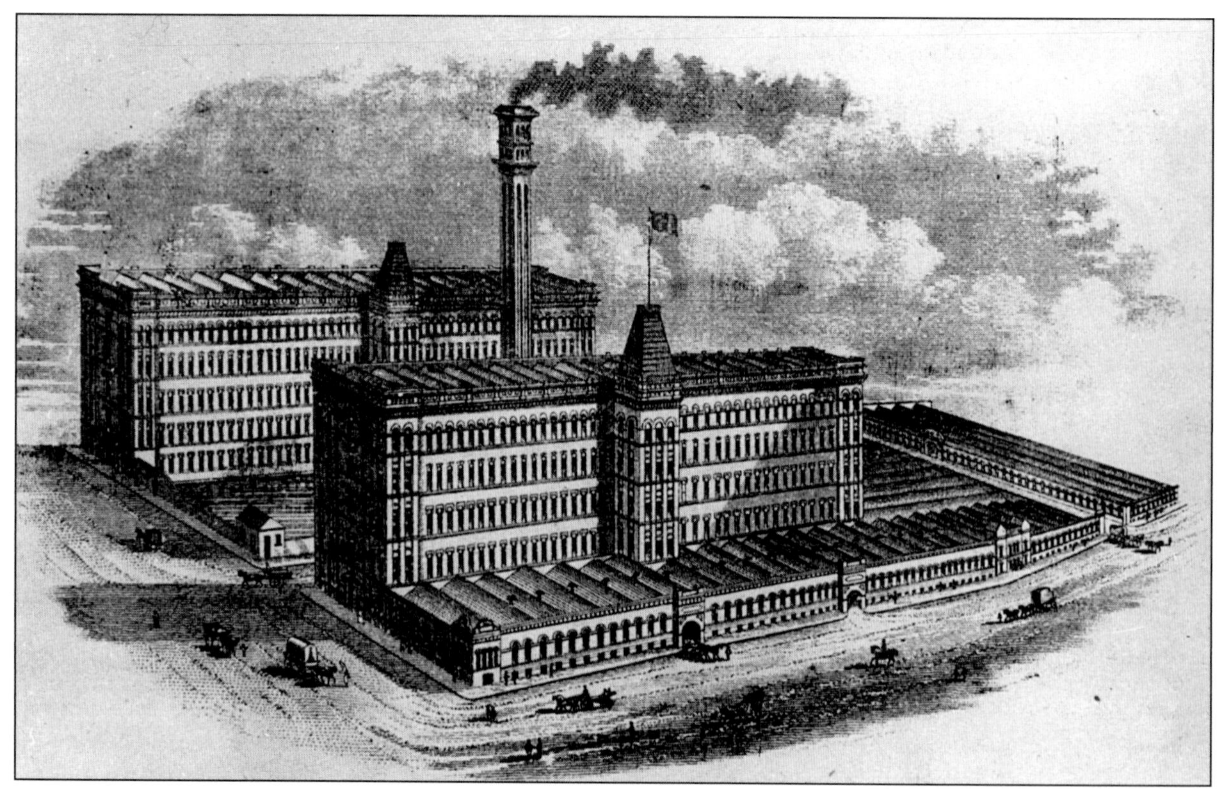

The famous Manningham Mills. *(Bradford Libraries)*

Manningham Old Hall, *c.*1863. *(Bradford Libraries)*

Cartwright Hall in Lister's Park, *c.*1904. *(Bradford Libraries)*

Church Street, Manningham, photographed in the early 1970s. *(Mabel Bruce)*

Bradford Children's Hospital, St Mary's Road, Manningham, opened in 1890 and believed to be the last surviving children's hospital with circular wards. *(Bradford Libraries)*

# Thackley

BACK in the 18th century, Thackley consisted of just a few houses and was described as a hamlet. Its name is derived from the act of gathering reeds and rushes to thatch or 'thack' homes and the stretch of waste or common land where the 'thack' was taken was known as the 'thack lea' or meadow.

In the 19th century, however, two major railways were built. The Midland's main line from London through to Scotland went along the top side of Thackley from Leeds to Skipton, then north. The Great Northern line from Bradford to Windhill followed a similar direction along the top end before its closure in 1964. The work on the railways brought more people to Thackley. Many intended to stay only temporarily but some remained with their families and so Thackley grew into a working village.

Today, a busy main road runs through Thackley, providing access to Shipley, Bradford and Leeds and, though the traditional village feel of the place has diminished, there remains quite a strong sense of place and community spirit among the inhabitants. Many of the oldest buildings still remain. The cottages on Windhill Old Road, for example, were once the workhouse, built in 1765 at a cost of £104 with room for 100 people. According to Cudworth, the workhouse was used by 20 townships, including Yeadon and Headingley. It was vacated when the new Union house at Clayton was built in 1858. Thackley Board School, built in 1883, is still standing and still used as a school, Thackley Primary and Nursery School. In 1968, it underwent a £57,000 modernisation and remodelling scheme, including additional windows, building extensions and oil-fired central heating. The old open fires, which used to heat the classrooms, have long gone, although apparently they were once used by teachers to cook their dinner over the fires while teaching. John Braine, author of *Room at the Top* (also filmed in and around Bradford), was educated here. During his childhood he lived in Harehill Road and then at 720 Leeds Road, Thackley, and used to play with his friends in Buck Wood, Ella Carr and Mally Hutton fields. In 1933 he won a scholarship to St Bede's Grammar and his name was inscribed in gold lettering on the Honours Board at Thackley School.

Another notable school in Thackley was Bradford's first open air school. Between the wars, the only possible cure for delicate children with TB with no antibiotics was thought to be sunlight and fresh air, as well as cod liver oil, breathing exercises and sunray treatment. The school was opened in 1908, adjoining Buck Woods and off Ainsbury Avenue. Children stayed the week and went home each Saturday for the weekend. The school was burnt down in 1966, after which the buildings were too badly damaged to use again.

Another building, the Great Northern, a large pub named after the railway, used to be an old hotel which provided accommodation for travellers coming into Thackley Station, which was situated behind the pub. At the back of the pub car park, the old railway course can still be seen, together with a stone bridge and the old station house.

There are still well-used local shops existing alongside the new Sainsbury's. Only recently, this included Jolene's Trading Post, which was remarkable in its popular retail of 'Wild West' memorabilia. The shop was owned by Cochacachanah, meaning 'White Antelope by

The Great Northern Pub, Thackley. *(Ann Birdsall)*

the Shining Water', a member of the Cheyenne American Indian tribe whose English name is Christine Godding. Christine was born in Thackley but acquired her title after meeting a group of Cheyenne Indians at a western event in Halifax in the 1980s. Her husband, Ted, used to wear a stetson in the shop and for a while the shop attracted many visitors to Thackley, in search of native American clothing and country and western wear.

Many of the green fields may have been lost to new housing and the encroachment of Idle on the one side and Windhill on the other, but Thackley still has a semi-rural setting with pleasant walks along the Leeds-Liverpool Canal at the lower end of the village. Both cricket and football clubs continue to flourish and be supported by their community. In 1995, fire seriously damaged the 47-year-old 100-seater wooden stand at the Ainsbury Avenue ground, but locals rallied round and helped to raise the £40,000 required to replace it. It is this community spirit which helps to renew the village feel of Thackley, which happily still seems to pervade in the 21st century. The Idle and Thackley Heritage Group is currently constructing its own website and has just published a history of Idle transport.

**Further Reading**

**Colehan, Philip** 'On the Way to the Top: John Braine's Bradford' *in* **Bob Duckett (ed.),** *Aspects of Bradford* Wharncliffe Publishing, Barnsley, 1999.

**Cudworth, William** *Histories of Bolton and Bowling* Thos. Brear and Co. Limited, Bradford, 1891.

**Cudworth, William** *Round About Bradford,* Queensbury, Mountain Press, Bradford, 1968.

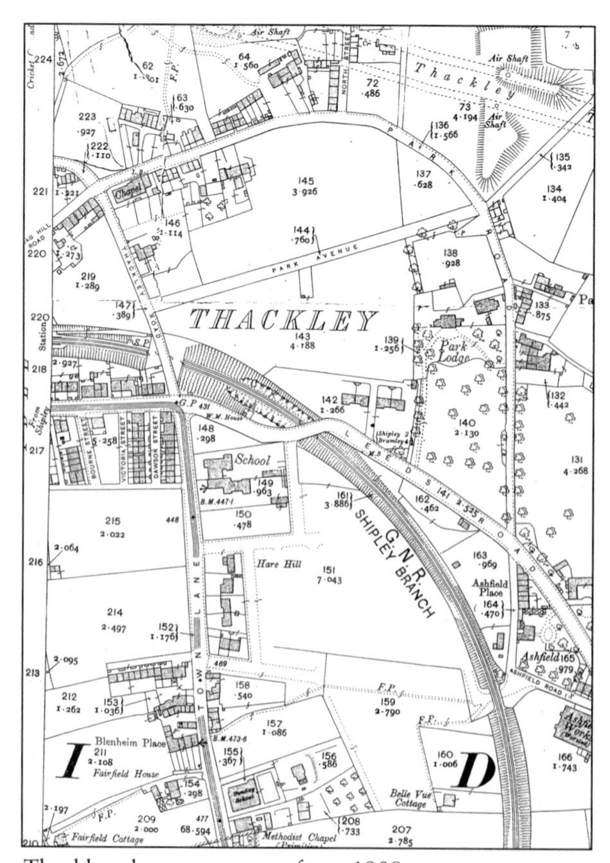


Thackley shown on a map from 1908.

A notable school in Thackley was Bradford's first open-air school. The school was opened in 1908, adjoining Buck Woods and off Ainsbury Avenue. Children stayed the week and went home each Saturday for the weekend. *(Bradford Libraries)*

The old railway bridge behind the Great Northern Pub, Thackley. *(Gina Szekely)*

Thackley Primary and Nursery School, formerly Thackley Board School. *(Gina Szekely)*

Old cottages, Windhill Old Road, Thackley. *(Gina Szekely)*

# THORNBURY

THORNBURY is situated to the east of Bradford, on the border with the city of Leeds. The area used to be owned by Thomas Thornhill, Squire of Calverley, up until his death in 1844. The land was then disposed of under the Thornhill Trustees Estate Act. Most of the buyers of the land were businessmen who built their own homes on the deserted moorland. By 1860, Thornbury had become a small hamlet consisting of around 10 houses. The hamlet did not have an official name, although it was commonly known as Calverley Moor, a name given to it by passing stagecoach drivers. The actual name Thornbury was apparently agreed upon by some of the residents of the village.

In 1882, Thornbury was incorporated into Bradford, finally losing its associations with Calverley. It gradually grew into a large residential area between Bradford and Leeds, famed nowadays for its huge roundabout. The roundabout itself consists of a large expanse of green land, situated at the busy junctions of Bradford Road, Leeds Road, Leeds Old Road and Dick Lane.

The roundabout sits exactly at the boundary between Leeds and Bradford and has been the centre of much speculation over the years. It was actually given to the district by Leeds Council for use as an open space. Residents today like to look out over the expanse of green land, and children regularly play on it. However, in the 1990s the people of Thornbury had to campaign against plans by Bradford Council to sell off the land for development.

They believed the busy roundabout would be made even worse if developers were allowed to build factories or offices on the land. They finally won the battle when the council approved plans to keep the site for open space and recreational use only.

Development has taken place however, just off the roundabout, with the construction of a huge multiplex cinema. The Odeon opened in July 2000 on the Gallagher Leisure Park, despite opposition from some residents.

Another new development in the area was the Thornbury Centre. In 1991 the former church of St Margaret's, that had stood on the site at Leeds Old Road since the last century, was declared unsafe and bulldozers moved in. The church members retreated to the adjoining dilapidated church hall building. There was now a need for a meeting place for the whole community, a place where everyone was accepted and welcomed regardless of background or race. This was especially important due to the mix of white and Asian populations in Thornbury.

From 1991 to 1995 the church ran meetings, social events and a range of community support from their humble base. However it was clear that much more was possible. Thus at the end of that period the parochial church council members decided to commission a feasibility study for their derelict site. With the support of the Bradford Metropolitan Council, the Bradford Diocese, the adjacent primary school and other local activities an initial National Competition was held to find an architect. By 1998 the Millennium Commission had committed to the project with further funding coming from the PCC of Bradford, the Diocese of Bradford, the Church Urban Fund, ERDF and English Partnership, as well as others. The total project cost of £2.7 million had been secured. The centre was officially opened by

The Thornbury Centre, 2001. *(Lesley Walker)*

Princess Alexandra on 13 April 2000. The centre has a café, bar facilities, a library, a new church, meeting rooms, a conference centre, a nursery and children's play areas. Courses and workshops are also run. There is something for all ages and abilities.

Unlike the Millennium Dome, the Thornbury Centre is clearly meant to last. This is an invaluable asset, both architecturally and socially, to this impoverished area of Bradford. It is likely to remain for many years, one of the most significant buildings for miles around.

The new Odeon Cinema at Gallagher Leisure Park, 2002. *(Gina Szekely)*

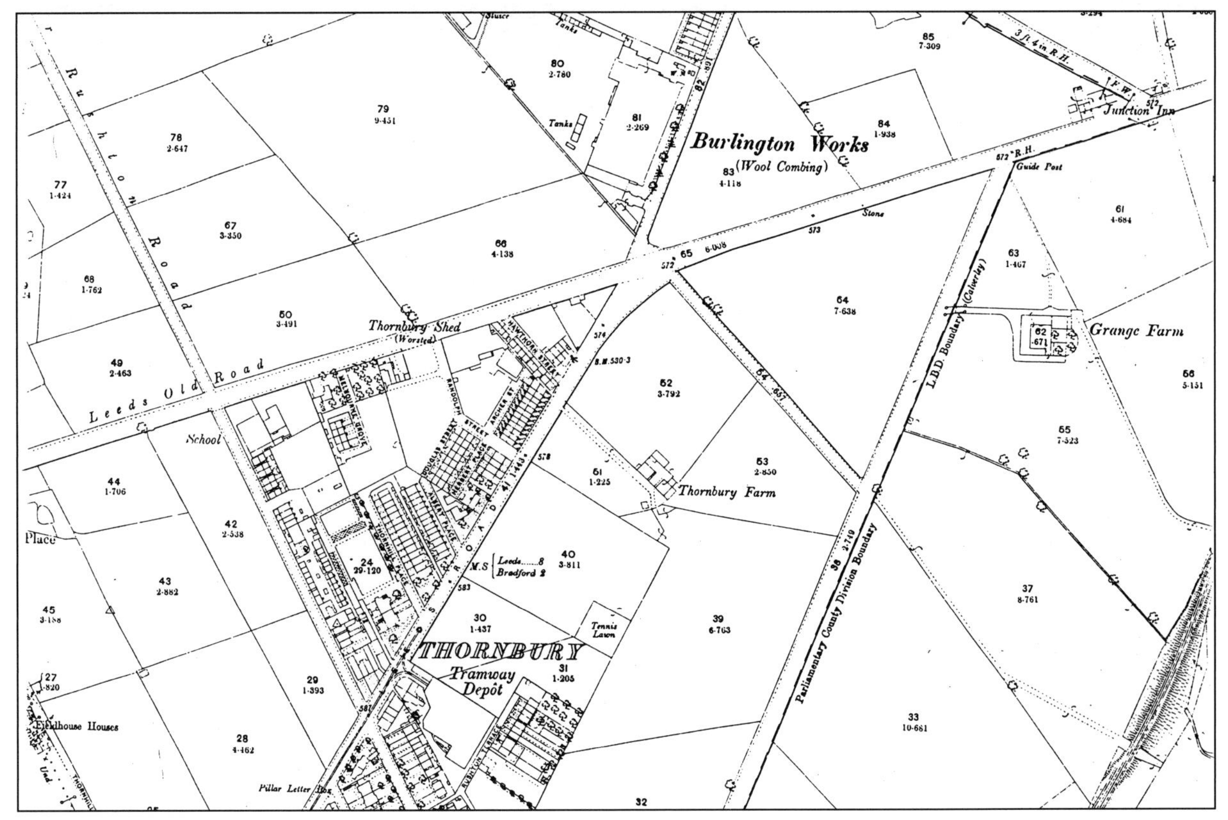


Map of Thornbury, 1893.

# THORNTON

THORNTON appears in the Domesday Book as Torenton (enclosure of thorns), a small hamlet to the west of Bradford held under the Manor of Bolton. Funeral urns dating back even further have been found in the area, indicating that some form of settlement has been there for a very long time. As early as 1150 Thornton was acquired by a family who took their name from the place. The Thorntons held the manor until one Roger de Thornton died without heirs, when it passed into the hands of the Bolling family (of Bolling Hall in Bowling). Sir Richard Tempest acquired the manor by marriage before it passed through the hands of the Midgeley family, John Cockroft, Attorney of Bradford and a Mr W.S. Stanhope. The manor was effectively dispersed by the Enclosure Acts of the early 1770s in which over 900 acres of moor and wasteland was enclosed.

Thornton grew slowly around and along the Bradford to Halifax Road, and as recently as 1800 there were less than 25 houses in the village. Alan Whitworth in his *Thornton in Times Past* tells us that three of these houses were pubs. Descriptions of Thornton are varied and at times quite contradictory. William Scruton in *The Brontës* said that 'The general aspect of this village ...is bleak and wild, ungraced by trees.' Mrs Gaskell said much the same in *The Life of Charlotte Brontë*, whereas Mr Leyland in *The Brontë Family* found it to be 'beautifully situated' with 'green and fertile pastures' and 'wooded dells with shady walks beautify and enrich the district.' Beauty really is in the eye of the beholder!

Thornton remained almost untouched by the events that shaped the future destiny of the country. The Civil War, which had a significant impact on nearby Bradford, seems to have passed Thornton by almost completely, and little recorded evidence about the place in the 16th and 17th centuries appears to have survived. No special significance, therefore, can have been attached to the arrival in Thornton, in 1815, of an Irish-born curate, his wife and two young children, to take up the post of perpetual curate at the Old Bell Chapel. That curate was Patrick Brontë, and during the five years he and his family lived at Thornton four further children were born – Charlotte, Branwell, Emily and Anne, who were to become known as possibly the most famous

Cottages, Thornton. A sense of remoteness from Bradford has long existed within Thornton. *(Pete Walker)*

literary family in the world. In 1820 Patrick took up a post at Haworth, a name perhaps more readily associated with the Brontës, but the five years spent at Thornton have brought a degree of fame to the place, along with visitors from across the world.

The 19th century saw much growth in Thornton. Sandstone was in great demand as Bradford built its mills, warehouses and villas for the newly rich wool barons, and Thornton was lucky enough to have large quantities of material, which could be quarried relatively easily. By the 1870s there were around 30 quarries in the area and small communities had sprung up around some, complete with strange, exotic names such as Moscow, Egypt and the forbidding World's End. As a direct result of all this quarrying, Thornton gained some of its more unusual features. In order to get rid of the vast quantities of waste produced by the digging some of the mining companies built huge walls and then back filled them with detritus, creating imposing features such as the aptly named Walls of Jericho, which loomed 30ft high on either side of Egypt Road.

The birthplace of the Brontës. *(Pete Walker)*

In 1865 Thornton got its own local board to oversee the affairs of the township. A gas supply was brought via the Clayton, Allerton and Thornton Gas Company, and the railway network reached Thornton in the mid-1870s

The centre of the village. Thornton retains a true village air. *(Pete Walker)*

Pupils at a Thornton school, thought to be the board school, 1910. *(Bradford Libraries)*

with the opening of the township's station on the Bradford, Halifax and Keighley Railway. Thornton Mechanics' Institute was erected in 1870, St James's Church (which replaced the Old Bell Chapel) two years later. The coming of the railways brought another impressive landmark to the Thornton area, in the shape of the huge viaduct, which spans the Pinch Beck Valley. Three hundred yards long, 120ft at its highest point and with 20 arches, this magnificent structure was built in the mid-1870s using local stone. Sadly the viaduct fell into a state of disrepair after the closure of the railway and was the subject of much debate in the 1980s when it was revealed in the local press that it had become a favourite haunt of vandals who were pushing huge stones into the fields below. Plans were drawn up to repair the damage and seal the ends of the viaduct, a listed building, which still looms large over the valley.

Along with much of the rest of the Bradford district, Thornton was involved in the worsted trade and several mills were built in and around the township. A look at the 1893 Ordnance Survey map of the area shows Thornton Mills on West Lane, Old Mill, just off Thornton Road, Dole and Prospect Mills also on Thornton Road as well as Albion Mills situated further out of town. Coal mining was also a noted business in Thornton in the late 1800s as the township lay on a seam of coal and fireclay.

In 1899 Thornton, along with Eccleshill, Idle, Tong and North Bierley, was incorporated into the ever-expanding city of Bradford, losing control of its own affairs, but due to its perceived remoteness from its new master, retaining its sense and spirit of independence. The 19th century had seen development and expansion in Thornton. The township had gained fine facilities and buildings, its affairs were looked after by a board of local people and it was described at the time as a 'healthy, thriving village'.

The 20th century saw many changes to

A tram from Bradford arrives in Thornton in the early years of the 20th century. *(Bradford Libraries)*

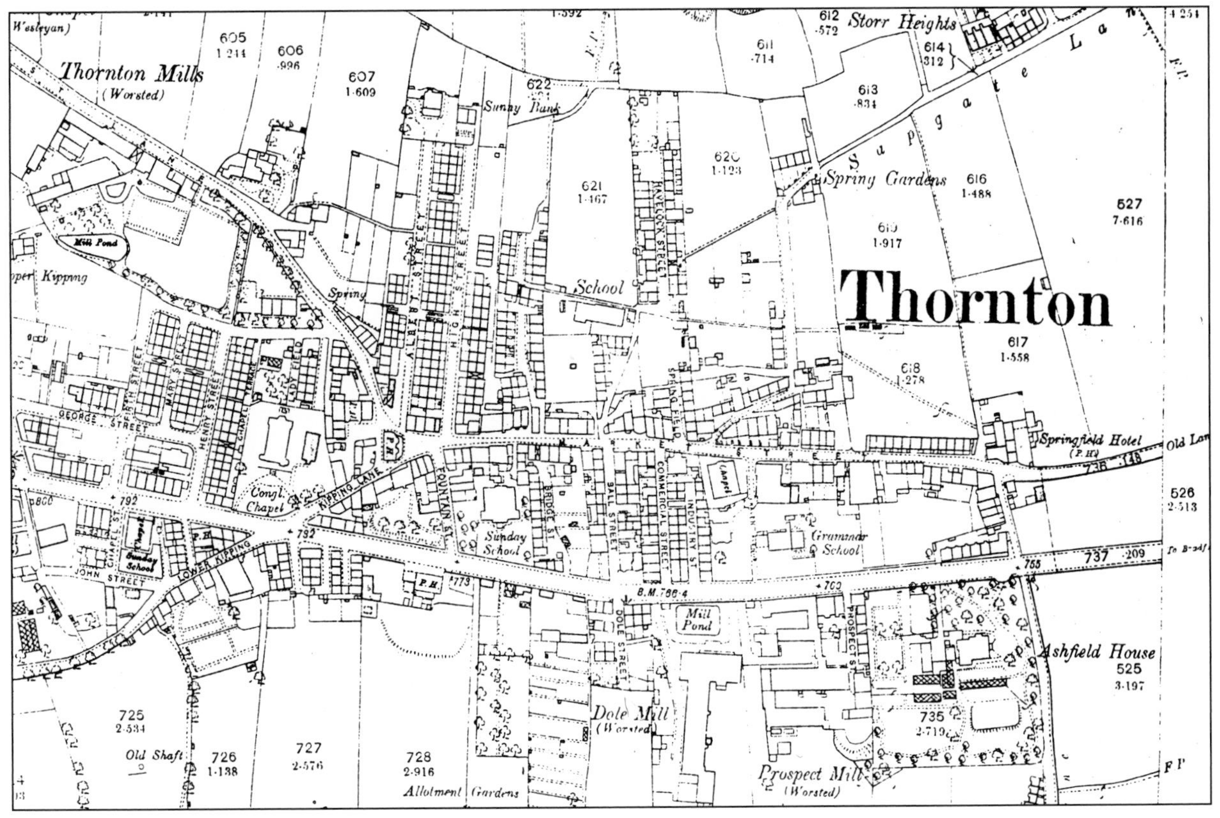


Thornton shown on a map from the 1890s.

This oddly shaped property, seen here in 1971, is known as 'coffin-end house', for obvious reasons. *(Jack Booth)*

Thornton, as it did to virtually every other district within Bradford. Times were changing and many facilities and amenities once seen as essential to a community were now seen as expensive and unnecessary. In 1964 the rail link to Thornton fell victim to the axe wielded by Dr Beeching, and the Mechanics' Institute building was lost to the bulldozers of Bradford Council in 1961. Thornton had gained its own swimming baths in the 1930s, which proved popular with locals, especially the youngsters, for many years. Unfortunately, despite a fierce local campaign, Bradford Council admitted that an estimated repair bill of over £800,000 on the dilapidated building was just too much and in January 2002 recommended closure.

Today Thornton retains something of an air of remoteness from Bradford, perched as it is on the hills at the end of the long Thornton Road, which rises out of the city centre. Market Street, its historic thoroughfare, has suffered over recent years as shops have been forced to close through lack of trade, some being replaced by flats. Many residents have expressed their views that a lack of investment in Thornton compared to other areas within Bradford has led to a steady decline in the village. Tourism has not taken off quite as much as was perhaps anticipated despite the birthplace of the famous Brontës taking pride of place on Market Street. Thornton's tale is not one of doom and gloom, however. A sense of community and belonging seems to prevail among many of its inhabitants, and the village itself is well served by its community centre, which incorporates the library and a medical centre, and excellent schools including the long established Grammar School where actress Billie Whitelaw was once a pupil. The cricket club and Conservative club provide entertainment, as do the village's pubs.

Thornton, then, remains in essence a true village. Not overly built up, with original features, self sufficient, and, as local historian Alan Whitworth put it 'almost scornful of the 20th century city of Bradford on its doorstep'.

**Further Reading**

**Whitworth, Alan** *Thornton in Times Past.*

# Tong

THE village of Tong lies on the outskirts of the Bradford district, several miles from the city centre. The dark tide of early Victorian industrialisation that so changed the landscape of the West Riding never quite reached Tong, so the village long retained its rural feel. It has been described as a quaint, linear village which lies among rolling fields, yet the problems of the 20th century are never far away, and Tong has suffered from increasing traffic volume and the problems which come with it.

Tong has long been settled, and the remains of a Saxon church have been found where St James's Church now stands, suggesting that the village may well have been among the first areas in the Bradford district to be used for religious worship. Norman stonework still exists within the modern church, which remains little changed since Sir George Tempest rebuilt it, in 1727.

The early history of Tong (Tuinc to the Saxons) is remarkably well recorded. The Domesday Book refers to a Henry de Tonge, and Cudworth, in *Round About Bradford*, mentions deeds and memorials, which name Richard de Tonge as holding the manor of Hugh Nevill, of Brearley, as lord of the fee. The Manor of Tong passed, by marriage, into the Mirfield family during the reign of Henry VI (1422–61). This family held the manor until Eleanor, daughter of one Christopher Mirfield, married Henry Tempest of Bracewell, during the reign of Elizabeth I (1558–1603). In 1664, Henry Tempest was bestowed with the title of baronet, and his descendants held the estate until Elizabeth Tempest married Thomas Plumbe, a rich merchant from the city of Liverpool. His son, John, assumed the name Tempest by sign-manual in 1824, and the estate remained in the hands of Tempests until Henrietta Tempest sold it off in 1940.

The family seat, Tong Hall, built in the Queen Anne style in 1702, lies adjacent to the aforementioned St James's Church. Cudworth tells the tale of how the hall's grounds were used for the 'coming of age' party for the young squire, John Tempest (d.1770). Oxen were roasted whole, and hogsheads of ale, brewed on the day John was born, were opened. The festivities were brought to a close by a foot race of 'Amazons', won by one Peg Mitchell, who was awarded a new holland smock for her efforts. The young squire did not have the best of fortunes in the future, however. He died young, a man of broken health and fortune, following a tragic incident in France, which had resulted in the death of a young lady who fell from a rope ladder while John was helping her to elope from a convent. John and his cohorts were arrested, and much of the estate had to be sold off in order to pay the heavy fines that were imposed. The aforementioned Mr Plumbe bought back the sold-off portions of the estate, and freed the remainder from the encumbrances placed upon them, thus restoring the estate to its former extent.

After Henrietta Tempest sold the estate off in 1940, Tong Hall briefly passed through private occupation before the Co-operative Youth Centres Ltd bought it to use as a residential educational facility. In 1951, the city of Bradford acquired the hall, and used it as a hall of residence for the Margaret McMillan College, as did the University of Bradford, between 1966 and 1974. A period museum was housed in the ground floor of the hall after Bradford Council reacquired the property in 1974, although this project was short-lived, the hall being put back on the market in 1977. It was eventually bought and converted into office accommodation, as it remains today.

The recent history of Tong village has not been without controversy. In the mid-1960s there was an abortive and highly controversial attempt by Bradford Council to allocate 375 acres of land in the area to provide a new housing estate for up to 12,000 people. The project failed when the then housing minister rejected the plans out of hand, following a fierce and sustained protest campaign by villagers. At this time, the village was described in the *Yorkshire Evening Post* as being a hamlet within a city, with a population of around 100. The article described how a 'workers' bus' took villagers to and from Bradford at the start and end of each working day, an extra bus running on Friday afternoons for the benefit of shoppers. Apart from this, villagers had to rely on their own forms of transport in order to reach the city.

The Local Government Commission on Boundaries suggested in the late 1960s that Tong should leave the wardship of Bradford, and move into the jurisdiction of nearby Pudsey. The village shopkeeper at the time, a Miss Alice Greenwood, summed up local feeling on the plan with typical Yorkshire bluntness – 'We should prefer to stay as we are', she said, adding 'we have an affection for Bradford'. So Tong remained as part of the city of Bradford, and life in the village, for the time being, went on as usual, unchanged and unhurried.

The council ward of Tong is definitely one of contrasts. It is a large ward, with a 1991 population of 14,106. It covers over five square miles, with the village itself lying towards its eastern edge, close to the Bradford/Leeds boundary. The ward also bounds Kirklees at its southern edge. Much of the ward remains rural, open country, yet it also includes two vast council estates (Holmewood and Bierley), and the Euroway Trading Estate.

Today, the village remains an excellent place to live, with all the usual facilities associated with modern life – shops, pubs and the famous Tong Garden Centre on Tong Lane. Plans were submitted to the council in January 2002 to convert part of the grounds of Tong Hall into a burial ground and garden of remembrance. The plans included brick-built vaults and a car park to be shared with the neighbouring St James's Church, whose vicar, Revd Gordon Dey, gave his full support to the plan. The hall's current owner, Paul Finn, who bought it from the council in 1990, announced that profits from selling plots in the grounds would be used to help restore the hall, which is still in use as business premises.

As close at it is to both Bradford and Leeds, Tong village retains something of its rural feel and could justly be considered one of Bradford's more pleasant suburbs. Its residents must surely feel privileged to live in such a pleasant location.

**Further Reading**

**Cudworth, William** *Round About Bradford,* 1876. (Reproduced 1968, Arthur Dobson Publishing Co.)

The interior of St James's Church, taken in 1977. *(Jack Booth)*

Another view of St James's Church, probably from the 19th century. *(Bradford Libraries)*

Ancient stocks at Tong. One wonders how many felons suffered punishment here. *(Jack Booth)*

Tenants of Tong Hall at the wedding of Sir Tristram Tempest, date unknown. *(Bradford Libraries)*

Tong Hall. This fine building, long the residence of the Tempest family, still stands proud in the village. *(Bradford Libraries)*

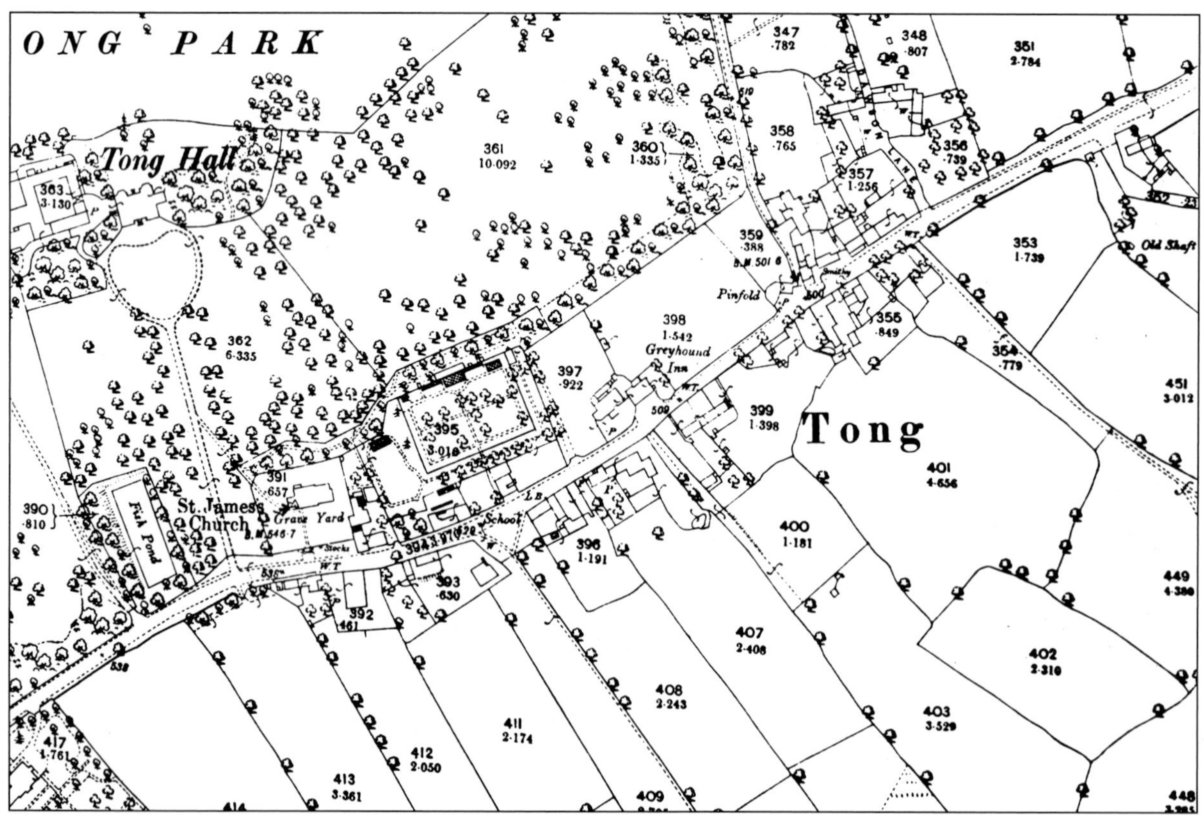


Tong shown on a map from the 1890s.

St James's Church, Tong, in 1971. The remains of a Saxon church were found on this site. *(Jack Booth)*

# Undercliffe

UNDERCLIFFE is set just to the north-east of the city centre of Bradford, its main artery being Otley Road. The first mention of the area was, according to C. Arthur Sugden, in 1418, when a man named Robert Leggard was up before the Bradford Court '...charged with having taken stone from the lord's soil, in his waste towards Undyrcliffe'.

The district was part of the moor of Bradford (now Bradford Moor). By 1611, Hundercliff, as it was then known, was a glebe in the West Riding of Yorkshire. On Johnson's map of Bradford (1802) most of Bradford Moor had been enclosed, and in the area of Hundercliffe the only buildings of note were a few farmhouses and Undercliffe House, built by John Hustler. By 1880 however, a great transformation had taken place in the area. Undercliffe House was now surrounded by buildings. Quarries had sprung up and buildings had appeared everywhere.

Undercliffe today is 600ft above sea level, higher than its original position. There is little doubt that the district got its name from the fact that the earliest settlements were built 'under-the-cliff'. But the village was 'forced up the hill'. The expansion of Bradford pushed the village further and further towards Eccleshill to where it is today.

Undercliffe was the setting for the legend of the famous Bradford boar. During the mid to late 14th century, there was a ferocious boar that lived in Cliffe Wood on the moors of Undercliffe. The boar frequently drank from a well in the wood. The boar terrorized the populace and caused much damage to land and property; so much so that the lord of the manor offered a reward for anyone brave enough to slay the boar and bring its head to the manor house. A hunter took up the lord's offer, and lay in wait near the well, ready to catch his quarry and thereby claim his reward. The boar duly arrived, and was shot by the hunter, who cut out the boar's tongue as proof of his victory and set off for the manor house. A little time later, another hunter, who had heard of the lord's offer, was passing through the woods and saw the slain boar lying near the well. Thinking of the reward he would receive, he cut off the boar's head and he too set off for the manor house. Arriving there before the true victor, he claimed his reward for having disposed of the ferocious creature, but was unable to account

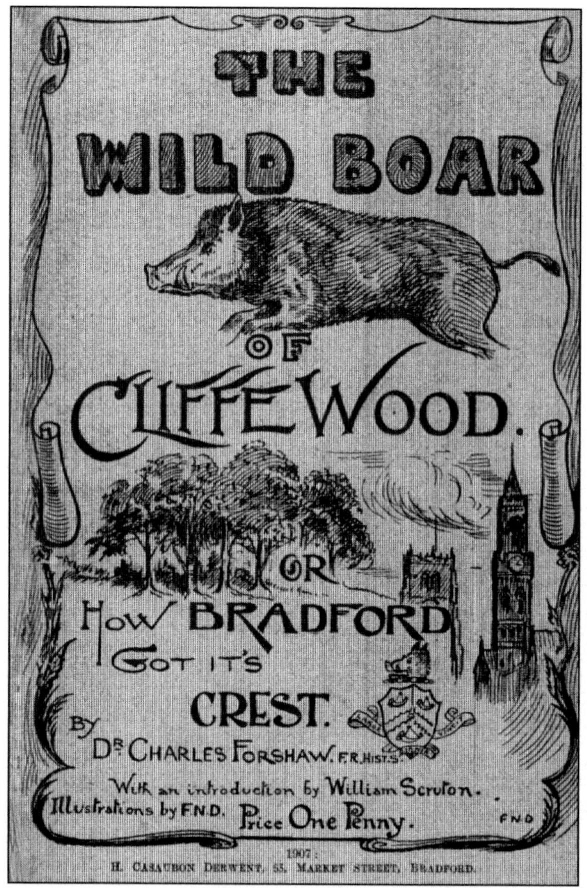

*The Wild Boar of Cliffe Wood.* Cover of a poetry book by Dr Charles Forshaw, 1907.

One of Undercliffe's busy main roads in 2002. *(Ann Birdsall)*

Some of the grand monuments at Undercliffe Cemetery. *(Bradford Libraries)*

for the boar's absent tongue. The first hunter then arrived and explained the true circumstances of the defeat, showing the boar's tongue as evidence of his veracity, and received his rightful reward; a plot of land called Hunt Yard in Horton.

Undercliffe today is renowned for its cemetery. It is possibly the most famous Victorian cemetery in Britain, outside Highgate in London. Wealthy Victorians often lived quite modest, unassuming lives, but when they died they certainly left behind the most flamboyant memorials. Similar to the Egyptians, they showed a desire to display strength and prosperity in life and immortality and eternity in the after-life. The cemetery itself is not huge (around 25 acres) but it is crammed with magnificent memorials and monuments to the dead, especially those of the rich mill owners, wool barons and politicians of the Victorian era. A walk round the cemetery today will reveal a mausoleum built like an Egyptian temple, complete with sphinxes, a Graeco-Roman temple with carved angels, and a Gothic steeple based on the Scott Monument in Princes Street, Edinburgh. These are just some of the grander monuments. There are hundreds of other interesting, if less grand, gravestones of ordinary Bradford people, including many who died in the wars that affected the city from the Crimea onwards.

The cemetery is set in a stunning location, with great views over the city centre and the city as a whole. It is not uncommon to see film and documentary crews at work in the grounds. Go and take a look some time. It is a place of peace and tranquility set amongst this bustling city.

**Further Reading**

**Sugden, A.C.** *Eccleshill and Undercliffe*, in **R.C. Allan** *The History of Bolton in Bradford-dale* Robert C. Allan, 1927.

**Beesley, I.** *Undercliffe. Bradford's Historic Victorian Cemetery* Ryburn Publishing, 1991.

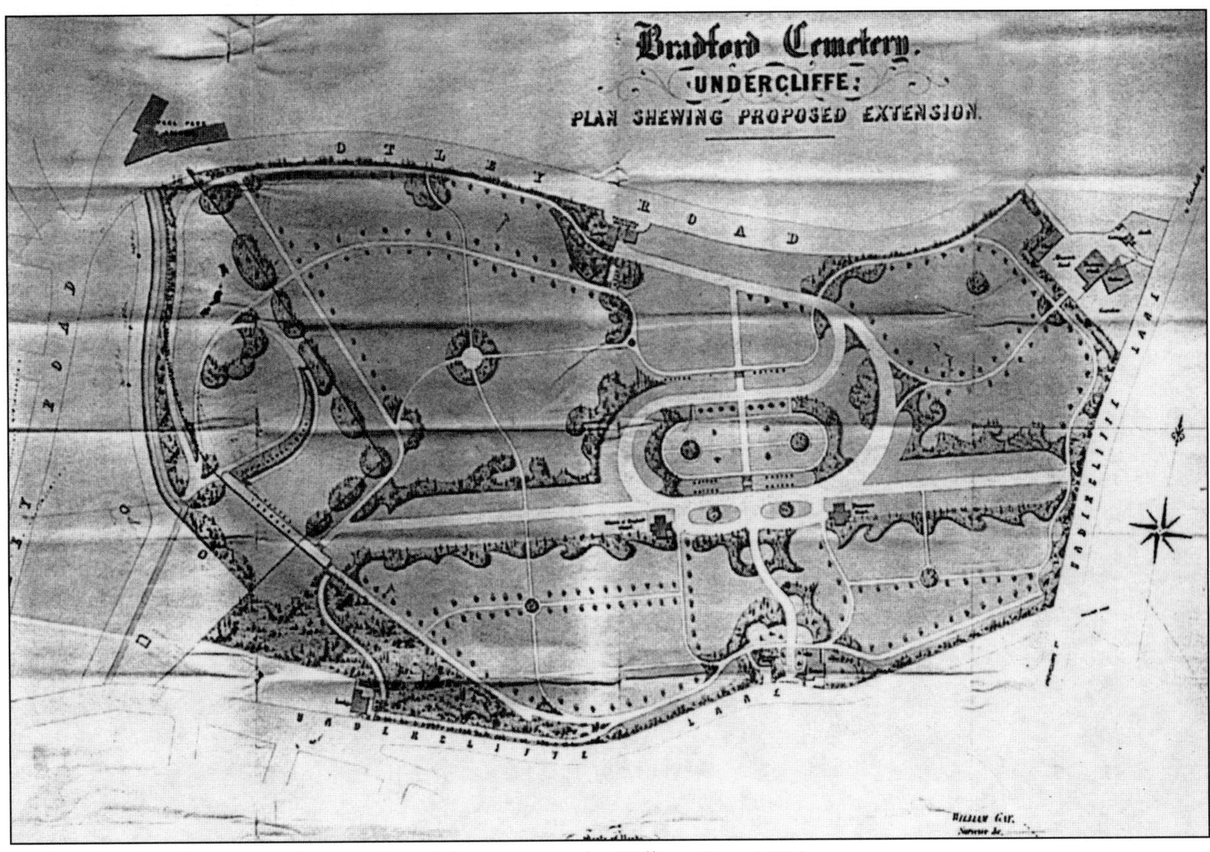


A plan showing the proposed extension of the cemetery, by William Gay, 1876.

Undercliffe Cemetery, from the *Illustrated Weekly Telegraph*, 1886.

Undercliffe Methodist Church, pictured in 1972. *(Bradford Libraries)*

Undercliffe Cricket Ground, Intake Road. This is the occasion of the Priestley Cup Final, Undercliffe v Bingley. *(Bradford Libraries)*

# WIBSEY

WIBSEY sits to the south-west of Bradford, at the top of one of the hills leading out of the city. The village actually stands at quite a height. Looking at an Ordnance Survey map, the 850ft contour line passes through the roundabout at the top of St Enoch's Road and the land rises to 975ft at Beacon Hill. This must be one of the highest extensive urban areas in Britain. The population in 1991 was 5,357.

The village was mentioned in the Domesday Book as Wibetese. At that time the manor was granted to Ilbert de Lacy by William the Conqueror. The origins of the village name are still uncertain. It has been suggested that the name is an adulteration of 'Wigbed's Land' or 'Wigbed's Height'.

The manor of Wibsey at that time had a common, and the village was surrounded by the Forest of Brianscholes. This was a dense, dark place which offered cover to wild boar and even wolves. Villagers had to have their wits about them on dark nights.

The manor was eventually taken over by monks from Kirkstall Abbey. The monks held the manor until around 1538, when the land was bought by William Rookes, two years before the dissolution of the monastery. The monks actually established the famous Wibsey horse fair. Drovers came here from all four corners of the British Isles to buy and sell horses. The fair's heyday seems to have been at the start of the 20th century, before the start of World War One. Horses were run along Fair Road, Folly Hall Road and Reevy Road. Additional markets selling various goods spread down Market Street, High Street and Smithy Hill, and even into the fields to the south of the village. You could buy anything from pots and pans to the famous Wibsey geese. There were also traditional fairgrounds, spectacularly lit at night. Much safer to wander around at this time than when the village was surrounded by the forest. The fair usually lasted from 5 October to 20 November. The final day was known as the 'Ketty Fair', on which all the horses and animals in poorest condition were sold off.

Wibsey Slack was home to the famous geese. They used to roam here quite freely and unconfined. It used to be regarded as a sign of impending bad weather if the geese left the slack and wandered into the actual village.

One of Wibsey's most pleasant areas is its park. It is around 30 acres in size and was opened on 25 May 1885, after a grand ceremony. It has always been a popular recreational area with locals. There are sports pitches, a lake, flower gardens, children's areas and an aviary. The park was once home to a strange attraction. In the 1930s visitors to the park were invited to relax in a 'sitting room' sculpted from plants and hedges. This novel arrangement was one of many sculptures produced by the first park keeper, James Walton.

Wibsey Park was built on Wibsey Slack. The area was to be enclosed by the lords of the manor in 1881, but a local councillor, Enoch Priestley, fought against this for the rights of the local people. The land was saved and the park created. Enoch Priestley became a local hero. He also campaigned for a new road linking the village to Bradford. When the road was completed Priestley was unofficially canonised by the locals. They named the road St Enoch's in his honour.

Wibsey has had a varied industrial history. It was a popular coal mining area, though it seems the coal was of poor quality and was only mined near the surface. The Industrial Revolution arrived here in 1836 with the opening of the first mill. One of the famous characters of this time was Joseph Hinchcliffe. He ran the Horton House Academy and in 1826 started up a Sunday School in the old chapel on Chapel Fold. The school had over 100 pupils and helped boys and girls whose religious instruction would otherwise have been neglected. Hinchcliffe carried out his teachings until ill health forced him to retire in 1834. However, no one came forward to replace him in the Sunday School, so rather than let the children down, Hinchcliffe decided to carry on teaching them from his home at Horton House. He was also a generous man. Every Christmas he treated the children to a Christmas dinner and each winter he would go round to the homes of the more needy boys and girls and instruct their parents to buy them new clothes at his expense. A true Samaritan of his day!

Today Wibsey is a popular commuter suburb for the city. The past seems to rub shoulders with the present here. Cobbled streets and ancient cottages still exist, many bearing the dates of when they were built. Wibsey has its modern face too. It has a thriving nightlife, based on the many pubs on the High Street, such as the Ancient Forresters, Malt Kiln, Swan and the Windmill. People travel from all over Bradford and from further afield, for a night out here. The village has all the shops and services you could wish for, mostly situated along the High Street. In fact you could live here quite comfortably without ever having to visit Bradford. This has helped Wibsey maintain a 'village' feel, even though it is only a few miles from the city centre.

**Further Reading**

**Carpenter, S.** *The manor of Wibsey; the town and district,* Bradford Libraries, 1992.

**Cudworth, W.** *Round About Bradford,* Thomas Brear and Co., 1876.

**Parker, J.** (1902) *Illustrated history of Wibsey, Low Moor, Oakenshaw, Wike, Norwood Green, Judy Brig, Royds Hall, Coley and Shelf,* Volume 2, J. Feather and Sons.

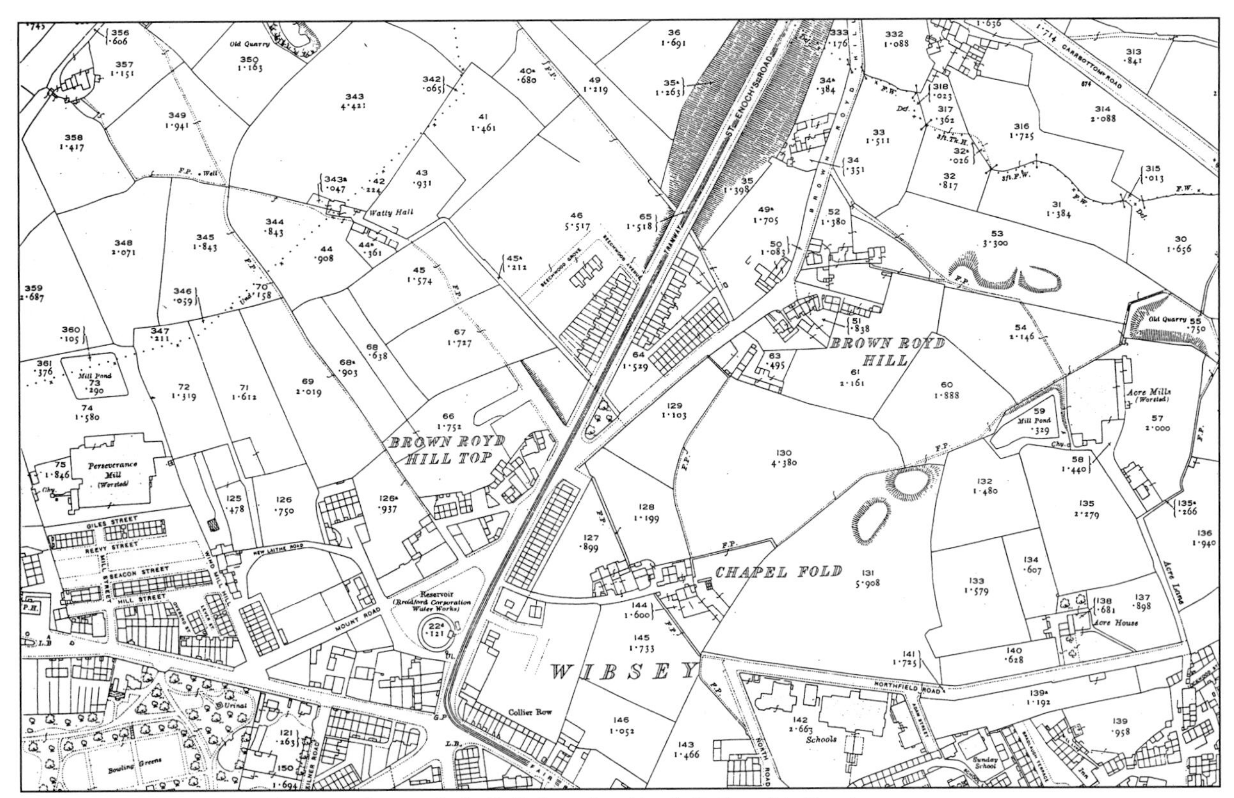


Map of Wibsey, *c.*1921, showing the newly built link to Bradford, St Enoch's Road.

High Street, Wibsey, *c.*1900. *(Bradford Libraries)*

The top end of St Enoch's Road, 1972. Named after Wibsey's unofficial canon, Enoch Priestley. *(Jack Booth)*

Wibsey Park floral organ, July 1928, designed by James Walton. *(Bradford Libraries)*

A winter scene in Wibsey Park, 1972. *(Jack Booth)*

Wibsey's busy High Street, 2002. *(Pete Walker)*

# Windhill

WINDHILL stands on the main Leeds road, out of Shipley. Its population in 1991 was 4,497. The name is intriguing. It obviously conjures up images of windswept moors. Its name would not be out of place in Brontë country. William Peel, a historian of Windhill Crag, believed the area got its name from a hill at the junction of Airedale and Bradford Dale. This hill was entirely unsheltered from the south-west wind and hence the area became known as Windhill. Cudworth, on the other hand, was more inclined to believe that the name was a derivation from 'winding hill' or 'whin hill'. Nowadays, no one seems to delve very deeply into the origins of the name. Most people seem to accept the first theory, that it is literally a windy hill, open to the elements and to the full force of all the winds blowing through the Pennines, down the Aire Gap.

In deeds going back to 1565, the hamlet was called 'Windell'. Around this time, the hillside, covered in woods and dominated by a range of rocks overlooking the valleys, must have been a magnificent and romantic sight. In the valley, the waters of Bradford Beck, then a powerful and pure source of water, attracted a number of iron smythies. However, lack of 'cole' or iron-ore speeded up their demise. Windhill then consisted of maybe half a dozen houses.

Windhill really started to prosper as a town with the arrival of the local woollen trade, in the late 18th century. In fact, Windhill is a perfect example of the growth of a manufacturing hamlet. By 1891 the population had risen to 6,730. This was in spite of the decline of the woollen industry. This had now been replaced by the worsted industry.

The town stood in an ideal position. It was at the junction of the Leeds-Liverpool and Bradford canals, and was bounded on the north by the River Aire. It even had its own railway station on the branch line of the Great Northern Railway to Laisterdyke.

Industrial housing sprang up all over the area, in quite a haphazard fashion. Many houses were built up on the crag, and in streets running up the hillside off Leeds Road. Many of these houses were back-to-backs and most had cellar dwellings.

In the 20th century, much of Windhill's housing fell into disrepair. Many of the dwellings became unfit for habitation and slums developed. In the middle of the century, a huge slum clearance programme took place. Between 1948 and 1968, around 950 homes were demolished. These were replaced by over 1,400 new houses, flats and maisonettes. The idea was to create a 'garden suburb'. This redevelopment led to the loss of many of Windhill's mills, chapels and other industries. In fact, the area's landmark school, library and public houses seemed to be the only buildings that remained. And these still remain today. Much of the old community was dispersed and the close-knit feel that once existed had all but gone.

Windhill was one of many districts which benefited from the generosity of the famous Scottish-American ironmaster, Andrew Carnegie. In 1903 his offer of £3,000 for the building of a library in Windhill was accepted. The Carnegie Library, at the junction of Leeds Road and Cragg Lane, was opened in 1905. Over the years, good use was made of the library and the meeting rooms situated above. The buildings still grace the main junction of Windhill, but have long since ceased to be the home of a library. Since the library's closure,

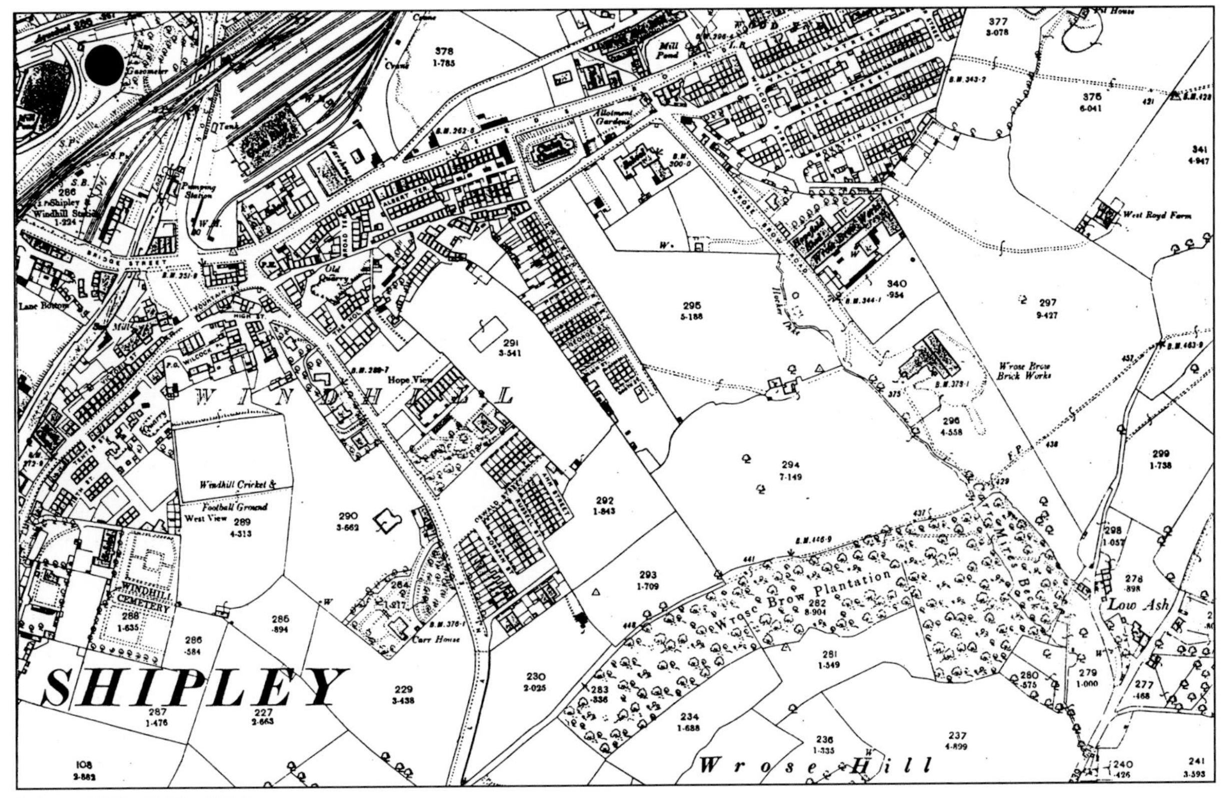


Map of Windhill, 1893.

they have been used as a dance hall, for an over-60s meeting place and even for wedding receptions. Today the Carnegie Library is occupied partly by a religious denomination.

One of the area's more famous thoroughfares is Digger's Hill. The official name for this steep, winding lane, linking Windhill with Shipley, is Cawcliffe Road. It was, and still is, a shortcut between the two districts. It seems that Cawcliffe Road earned its new name because of the amount of times that the road was dug up for repair. There seemed to be many burst water mains on the road and there were always workmen digging there. Hence the name 'Digger's Hill'. If it were to be nicknamed today for the same reason, the M1 might be a more suitable choice.

Windhill today is a shadow of its former self. Looking at its busy roads today, surrounded by modern housing and flats, it is impossible to see any evidence of the rows of back-to-back terraces, blackened by smoke. It is still a picturesque area though, with its views over the Aire Valley and across to Heaton and Northcliffe. It will always be a popular area to live, being ideally situated for commuting to Bradford, Leeds and Keighley. It may have lost its sense of community, but it remains a busy, popular suburb.

**Further Reading**

**Cudworth, W.** *Round About Bradford,* Thomas Brear and Co., 1876.

There are also many books on Windhill's history, including reminiscences, published by the Windhill Memories Group. The titles include: *Window on Windhill*; *Windhill Folk Remembered*; *Windhill Cragg*. They can be ordered directly from the group: Windhill Memories Group, Windhill Community Centre, Church Street, Windhill, Shipley, BD18 2NR

View looking over Windhill, 1988. *(Bradford Libraries)*

Hall Lane with Carr Lane in the foreground, 1967. The slum dwellings have been cleared to make way for new council flats. *(Bradford Libraries)*

Hall Lane, 1988. The council flats occupy the site of the former terraced dwellings. *(Bradford Libraries)*

Carnegie Library, Leeds Road, Windhill, 1968. *(Bradford Libraries)*

# Wrose

WROSE occupies a lofty position to the north of Bradford, overlooking Windhill, and boasts spectacular views across the valley to Manningham, Frizinghall and Heaton Woods. Shipley lies beneath Wrose Hill, and on clear days the views up the Aire Valley and beyond are breathtaking. Carr Lane snakes down from Wrose to Windhill, and must be one of the steepest roads in the entire district. Indeed, in times gone by, Wrose's elevated, breezy position made it almost unapproachable by vehicular traffic from the Shipley or Windhill areas. William Cudworth remarked in his 1876 book, *Round About Bradford,* that Wrose had made little headway since it was first surveyed in 1583 along with the rest of the lands and townships in the possession of the Earl of Cumberland.

Almost within living memory Wrose was still a small, farming community, originally consisting of a mere 31 houses. The old 'Wrose village', which now lies behind the Wrose Bull pub, off Wrose Road, is where some of these houses can still be found, clustered near to the old village green. Date stones on two of these buildings give an indication of how long the village has been there, showing 1616 and 1668 respectively. A much older building stood nearby until relatively recently. The structure, a mediaeval threshing barn, was located off Towngate, and was one of only a few such barns still in existence in Britain. The barn was in a very poor condition, however, and was pulled down in the mid-1990s, despite efforts by the Wrose Local History Group to save it. The site now houses a complex of flats for the elderly.

The green around which the village grew up was used as a thoroughfare, and by 1867 it had suffered so badly from the increasing volume of traffic, which had even found its way up the steep hills to Wrose, that urgent improvements had to be made to it. The villagers sought permission from the lord of the manor, a Mr W. Stansfield, and formed a committee to oversee the work. By way of a commemoration of this undertaking, an elm tree was planted, which was to become a much-loved focal point of the village, for over a century. Unfortunately, the tree had to be felled in March 2000 after it was discovered to be suffering from Dutch elm disease. Dozens of curious villagers turned out to see the tree felled and its roots dug out, to find out if there was any truth in the local legend that treasure was buried under it. Sadly, however, all that was found was a Victorian glass 'time capsule' containing little more than rotted down documents, probably newspapers. History turned full circle later in the same year, however, when pupils from the nearby Low Ash Primary School planted a new tree – complete with plastic time capsule! It is a nice thought, and altogether possible, that some of the children could well be descended from the villagers who planted the original tree, some 133 years previously.

Near to the green stands the popular Wrose Bull pub. This building was the manor house back in the 1700s and still has two cottages attached to it, now partly hidden by a much more recent extension. The building was the long-time home to the Dawson family and was opened as a pub in 1956, after the nearby Hare and Hounds was deemed too small to cater for Wrose's growing population. The brewery originally intended to call its new premises the Hare and Hounds, as the new pub was simply replacing the old one, but the locals got together and convinced them that the Wrose

Cottages, Low Ash Drive. The ancient village is still very much in evidence just off the busy Wrose Road. *(Gina Szekely)*

This property, seen *c.*1902, was for many years the residence of the Ward family, who were local grocers and general dealers. Built in 1616, the house still stands. *(Bradford Libraries)*

Wrose Hill Chapel, Low Ash Avenue, still very much part of village life. *(M. Birdsall)*

This picture clearly shows how Wrose occupies a lofty position, looming over Shipley, Windhill and Bolton Woods. *(M. Birdsall)*

Bull was a much better name. The bull in question was a prize bull that had been kept in a field behind the Hare and Hounds! The pub is a popular focal point for the village, and has been used as a meeting place for a variety of groups including Shipley's Twin Town Association.

Further along Wrose Road stands the Bold Privateer, the second of Wrose's pubs. Its name is a clear reflection of Wrose's history, being

Site of the 'Wrose Elm', planted in 1867. A new tree was planted in March 2000 by local school children. *(Gina Szekely)*

named after the third Earl of Cumberland and 13th Lord de Clifford who owned the village and took part in the fight against the Spanish Armada. In this time of pub closures, Wrose is lucky to be served by two such fine, lively and popular establishments.

Fields, farmlands and quarries once surrounded Wrose Road, along which Wrose now sprawls. One of these quarries supplied stone used in the construction of the Houses of Parliament. The road is now almost entirely surrounded by housing developments, including the Plumpton and Low Ash estates, although it does still boast a large, open space, used as a recreation ground. Just about all of Wrose's shops and amenities are spread out along this road, giving Wrose quite a linear feel. Wrose Road is unusual in that one half of it is in Shipley, with a BD18 postcode, and the other in Bradford, with a BD2 postcode, each half having its own numbering system – a postman's nightmare. The road, like many thoroughfares in the district, is now heavy with traffic and this has been a major gripe for villagers, as crossing it can be all but impossible at peak times.

The striking crucifixion scene outside the Church of Our Lady and St Anthony, on Wrose Road, was a landmark in Wrose for many years. The church, one of surprisingly many in the village, was pulled down in the 1990s, the site now being occupied by housing. Further along Wrose Road, past the Bold Privateer and the row of shops that houses the village's library, stands Wrose Community Centre. This building, built in the 1940s, is little more than an elongated shed, and was used as a maternity centre and health clinic until Wrose Community Association took it over in 1983. Many groups use the centre as a base, and it is a veritable hive of activity. Its shortcomings are all too obvious, though, and in late 2001 plans were laid to replace it with a new £350,000 structure which would house a main hall, offices and also, possibly, the village's library. The Community Association intended to apply for a National Lottery Community Fund grant to provide funding for a project that would inject a real sense of community togetherness and would be a wonderful focal point for the village.

Undoubtedly the biggest event in Wrose's calendar is the annual carnival, held on the first Saturday in July. The day includes parades, fairground rides and competitions, and is well attended both by Wrose residents and people from further afield, often attracting up to 5,000 visitors. In general, Wrose has a happy, welcoming feel to it and is seen as a good area to settle in, with stunning views at the 'old end' and a full range of shops and amenities to cater for one and all.

**Further Reading**

**Cudworth, William** *Round About Bradford,* 1876. (Reproduced 1968, Arthur Dobson Publishing Co.)

Wrose Community Centre was built in the 1940s. Clearly inadequate for modern needs, plans were drawn up in late 2001 for a replacement. *(M. Birdsall)*

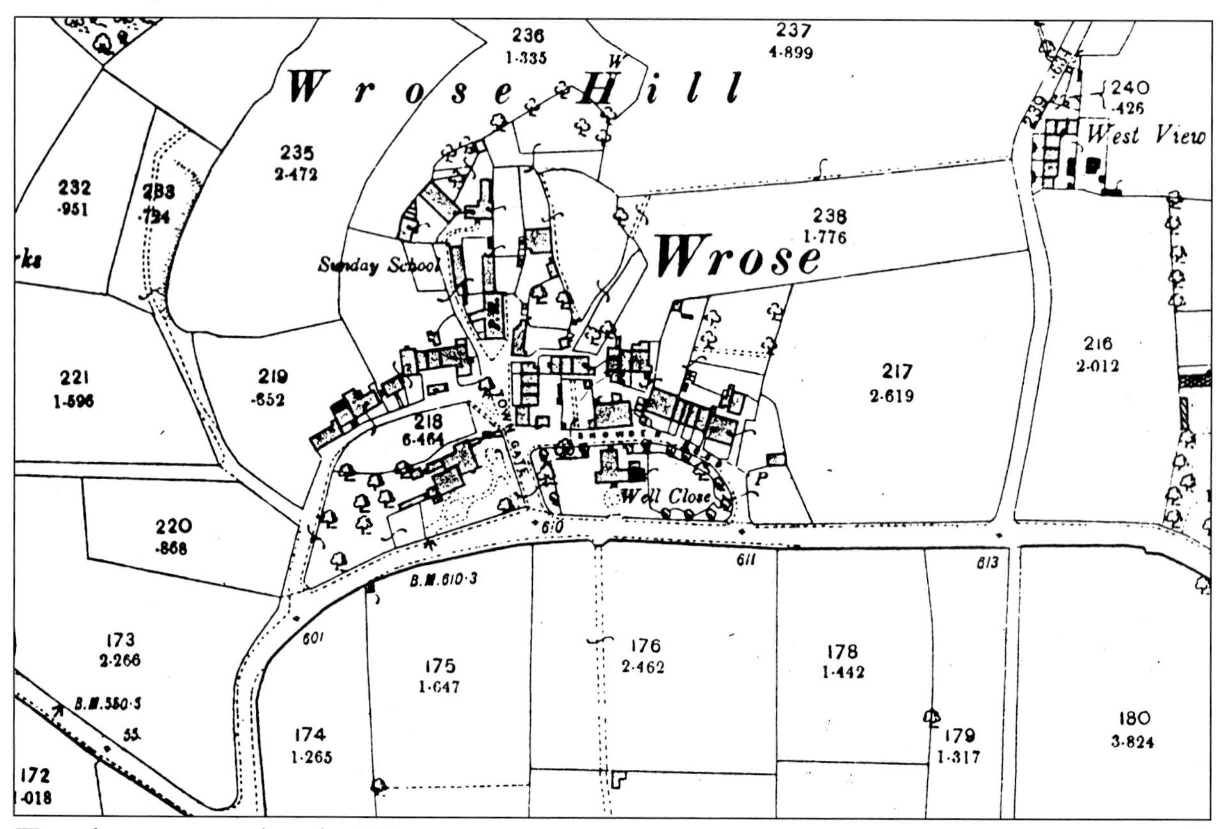


Wrose shown on a map from the 1890s.

# INDEX